ABRAHAM
and HIS SONS

BIBLE WISDOM FOR TODAY

ABRAHAM
and HIS SONS

JAMES HARPUR

RABBI JONATHAN ROMAIN
CONSULTANT

Reader's
Digest

The Reader's Digest Association, Inc.
Pleasantville, New York • Montreal

A READER'S DIGEST BOOK
Conceived, edited, and designed by
MARSHALL EDITIONS
170 Piccadilly, London W1V 9DD

PROJECT EDITOR: THERESA LANE
PROJECT ART EDITOR: HELEN SPENCER
PICTURE EDITOR: ELIZABETH LOVING
RESEARCH: JAMES RANKIN
COPY EDITOR: JOLIKA FESZT
INDEXER: JUDY BATCHELOR
MANAGING EDITOR: LINDSAY McTEAGUE
PRODUCTION EDITOR: EMMA DIXON
PRODUCTION: NIKKI INGRAM
ART DIRECTOR: SEAN KEOGH
EDITORIAL DIRECTOR: SOPHIE COLLINS

The publishers acknowledge Rabbi Jonathan Romain as author of
the "Messages for Today."

The acknowledgments that appear on page 96 are hereby made a
part of this copyright page.

Library of Congress Cataloging in Publication Data

Harpur, James.
    Abraham and his sons / James Harpur ; Jonathan Romain,
consultant. — 1st North American ed.
        p.   cm. — (Bible wisdom for today ; v. 4)
    Includes bibliographical references and index.
    ISBN 0-89577-959-5
    1. Abraham (Biblical patriarch) 2. Jacob (Biblical patriarch)
3. Joseph (Son of Jacob) 4. Patriarchs (Bible)—Biography.
5. Bible. O.T.—Biography. I. Romain, Jonathan A. II. Title.
III. Series.
BS580.A3H29   1997
222'.110922—dc21   97-12487

Origination by HBM Print, Singapore
Printed and bound in Italy by L.E.G.O. Spa.

Pictures shown on the preliminary pages: (page one) Lot
escaping from Sodom, from a 16th-century English
stained-glass window; (page two) a view of the Dead Sea,
in Israel; (page three) a 14th-century Italian relief of the
binding of Isaac; (page five) a 15th-century German
manuscript illustration of Jacob and Esau.

CONTENTS

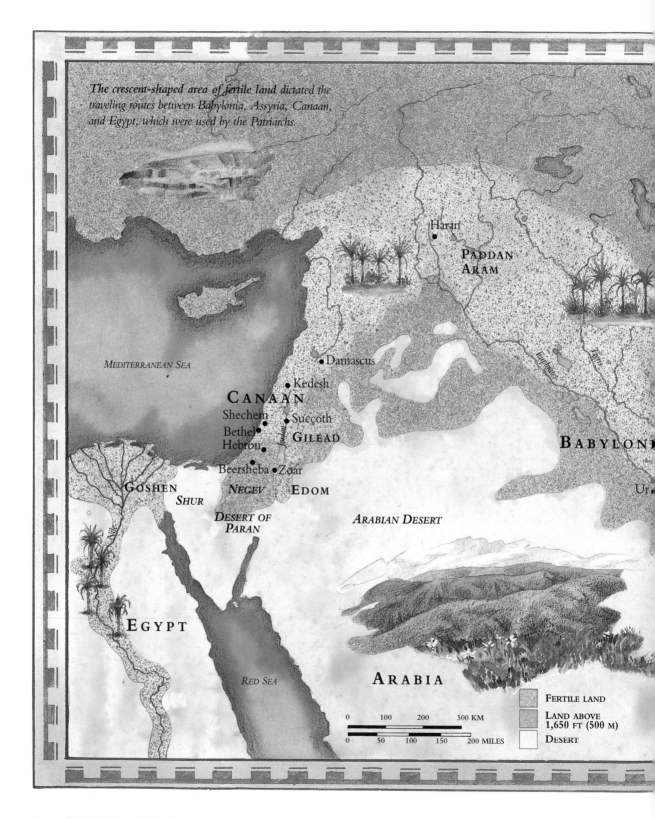

The crescent-shaped area of fertile land dictated the traveling routes between Babylonia, Assyria, Canaan, and Egypt, which were used by the Patriarchs.

Haran

PADDAN ARAM

Euphrates

Tigris

MEDITERRANEAN SEA

Damascus

Kedesh

CANAAN

Shechem

Succoth

Bethel

GILEAD

Hebron

Jordan

BABYLON

Beersheba

Zoar

GOSHEN

NEGEV

EDOM

Ur

SHUR

DESERT OF
PARAN

ARABIAN DESERT

Nile

EGYPT

RED SEA

ARABIA

	FERTILE LAND
	LAND ABOVE 1,650 FT (500 M)
	DESERT

0   100   200   300 KM

0   50   100   150   200 MILES

CASPIAN SEA

PERSIAN GULF

INTRODUCTION

At the heart of Genesis – the first book of the Bible – lie the lives and destinies of Abraham and his son Isaac, grandson Jacob, and great-grandson Joseph, as well as their families. These wandering Semitic farmers were the great ancestral father figures, or Patriarchs, of Israel. Their stories describe the origins of the nation of Israel and have been treasured by countless generations of Jews and Christians. The stories offer wisdom, honest descriptions of human failings and triumphs of faith, and evidence of the providential care of God. Central to the accounts is God's solemn pact, or covenant, with Abraham. By this covenant, God promised Abraham and his offspring that He would bless them, make them into a great nation, and give to them Canaan, the place later known as the land of Israel.

Genesis opens with a description of God's creation of the world and expulsion of Adam and Eve, the first humans, from the garden of Eden. The story unfolds of humanity's increasing wickedness and God's judgment, enacted in a universal flood. After the waters had subsided, only Noah and his family remained, with the animals God had told them to preserve. It was left to them to repopulate the Earth.

✡ The Patriarchs ✡

Beginning in chapter 12, Genesis focuses on a single family: Abraham and his offspring. Called by God, Abraham moved his household from Mesopotamia to Canaan, the Promised Land, where he lived out the remainder of his days. After Abraham's death, his son Isaac – mentioned only briefly – then Isaac's son Jacob, inherited God's covenantal promises.

Jacob, portrayed as a scheming liar, tricked his twin brother Esau out of their father's blessing. Because he feared Esau's vengeance, Jacob fled to Paddan Aram and the home of his uncle Laban, whose deviousness matched his own. Eventually, a wiser and more mature Jacob left Laban and headed back toward Canaan. During his journey, God renamed him Israel, the name

The symbols on the top of each page represent the Patriarchs. The Semitic nomads (p. 6) symbolize Abraham, the symbols of the 12 tribes of Israel (pp. 7–8) represent Jacob, and the Egyptian papyrus (p. 9) represents Joseph.

The Patriarch Abraham and his wife Sarah are depicted together, in this 17th-century Russian icon painting. The nation of Israel is descended from this couple, as promised in God's covenant with Abraham.

by which the Jewish nation subsequently would be known. Forgiven by his brother, Israel settled in Canaan with his two wives, Leah and Rachel, and his 12 sons – the ancestors of the 12 tribes of Israel – who inherited the promises of God's covenant.

From the story of Jacob, Genesis moves on to Jacob's second youngest and most beloved son – Joseph. Sold into slavery by his jealous brothers, Joseph rose from slave status to become the highest-ranking official in Egypt after the king, or pharaoh. Genesis presents Joseph as a wise, forgiving man who overcame his trials by relying on the guidance given through the Lord's providential care. Of major significance in the Joseph cycle of stories is the migration of Jacob and his family to Egypt to receive famine relief from Joseph's vast stores of grain. This event paved the way for the later enslavement of the Israelites and their eventual escape from Egypt to Canaan, retold in the Book of Exodus.

✡ The writing of Genesis ✡

Genesis and the four books that follow it are known as the Pentateuch ("five volumes"). They form the Law, or Torah, which is the cornerstone of Judaism. The authorship of the Pentateuch has traditionally been ascribed by Jews and Christians to Moses, the great leader who brought the children of Israel out of Egypt. Many scholars believe that the books began as oral traditions that were handed down from generation to generation. The stories were written down at various times in history, and eventually they were compiled into a body of work.

Through an analysis of writing styles, the use of specific terms, and duplications of stories, many scholars believe that the Pentateuch originated from four sources. Some also think that the books were given their final form after the Jews' exile in Babylon in 586 BC and that their purpose was to encourage and give guidance to Jews returning to the Promised Land. However, intensive literary and archeological research has called many of these theories into question.

Historical evidence of the existence of Abraham and the other Patriarchs has been elusive. Details in the stories suggest that they lived during the early centuries of the second millennium BC. Indeed, excavations at ancient Middle Eastern sites, such as Mari and Nuzi in the Mesopotamia region, have unearthed writing tablets that have shed light on aspects of patriarchal society and customs, including marriage, inheritance, and adoption. Details of Joseph's life in Egypt have been corroborated by archeology. For example, Pharaoh gave Joseph a gold chain and signet ring (Genesis 41:42) – objects known to be the emblems of high-ranking officials in later Egyptian history.

This book focuses primarily on Abraham and his male descendants, especially Jacob and Joseph, reflecting the fact that the world of the Patriarchs was a male-dominated society. ("Sons" is used in the broader sense of male descendants as a whole.) Men fulfilled the leading roles in social, religious, and political affairs with rare exceptions. Yet in the biblical stories to follow, many women, including Abraham's wife Sarah, her servant Hagar, and Jacob's wives Rachel and Leah, play crucial roles. Together, the men and women take part in the realization of God's promise to Abraham that his descendants would inherit Canaan. ▲

THE STORY OF ABRAHAM

The "FATHER of FAITH"
GENESIS 12–24

> " *'I will make you into a great nation and I will bless you; I will make your name great...'* "
> GENESIS 12:2

THE FIRST GREAT Patriarch of the Hebrews, Abraham is one of the major figures of the Bible, revered by Jews, Christians, and Muslims. Genesis records his life as a series of stories that illustrate both Abraham's personal relationship with God and the gradual evolution of his descendants into the people of Israel.

God made promises to Abraham that he would be the forefather of a great nation; that his descendants would become as numerous "as the stars"; and that they would inherit Canaan, the Promised Land. Since he was old and childless, and his wife Sarah was barren and past the age of childbearing, Abraham must have wondered how God could fulfill His promises. Perhaps because they lacked faith or patience, the couple arranged for Abraham to father a son, Ishmael, by his wife's maidservant Hagar. Then, at the age of 90, Sarah gave birth to Abraham's son Isaac, who became next in line to inherit God's promises.

The Patriarch Abraham is portrayed in his old age, in this detail from a 14th-century Italian fresco by Simone Martini.

Despite having occasional lapses in good judgment, Abraham became known as the "father of faith" because of his extraordinary obedience to the Lord's command. This is shown, for example, by his prompt departure from Mesopotamia when God called him to go to Canaan, a place he had never seen. But his faith passed the severest test of all when God commanded him to sacrifice his son Isaac. Committed to carrying out this grim action, Abraham was stopped by God from killing his son only at the last moment.

✿ The Promised Land ✿

Abraham continued to live in Canaan for the rest of his life. When Sarah died, he bought a cave and its adjoining plot of land, near the town of Hebron, as a tomb for her and, eventually, other members of his family.

This was the first time Abraham had legally acquired a piece of the Promised Land, the land his descendants would one day fully possess. When he died at the grand age of 175, Abraham was laid to rest in the cave, next to Sarah.

Genesis faithfully depicts Abraham's failings as well as his virtues. For example, in Egypt, where he and his family had traveled so that they could escape a famine, he presented Sarah as his sister to guarantee his own safety, thereby allowing her to be chosen by Pharaoh for his harem. Yet Abraham was a righteous man who showed compassion, for instance, in trying to persuade God to spare the people of Sodom and Gomorrah. A brave soldier, he rescued his nephew Lot from an invading army. Abraham was generous and hospitable – shown in his welcome for the three angels at Mamre. Most of all, he was wholeheartedly committed to God, prepared even to kill his own cherished son at the Lord's command. ▲

When Abraham was called by God, he and his family were living at Haran. He traveled to Shechem in Canaan, probably following routes established by merchants. At various times he also visited Egypt, Bethel, and Mamre (near Hebron).

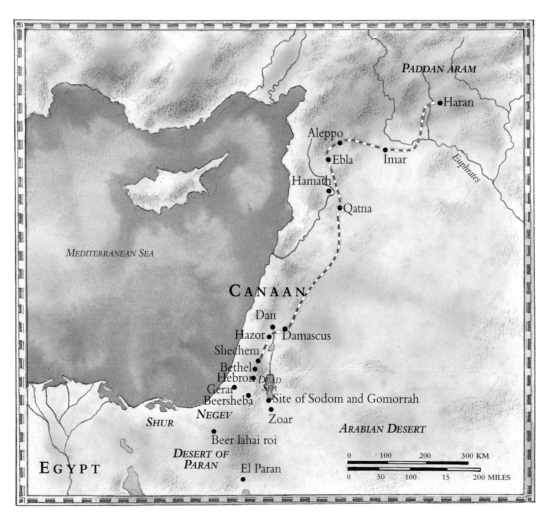

SUMMONED *by* GOD

The CALL *of* ABRAHAM
GENESIS 12–15

> " *'Leave your country, your people, and your father's
> household and go to the land I will show you.'* "
> GENESIS 12:1

Genesis introduces Abraham at the point when he received a revelation from God. It was the first of a number of divine encounters during his lifetime. At the time, Abraham was living in Haran, a town in Paddan Aram in northern Mesopotamia (modern Iraq), near the Euphrates River. His father, Terah, had brought him and the rest of the family there from the city of Ur, in southern Mesopotamia. God told Abraham to leave his home and go to a land that He would show him. He promised that He would make Abraham into a "great nation."

So, at 75 years of age, Abraham, with his wife and half-sister Sarah (called Abram and Sarai until Genesis 17), set off for Canaan. Traveling with the couple were Abraham's nephew Lot and their servants, flocks, and herds. When they arrived, the Lord appeared to Abraham at a place called Shechem and promised that He would give Canaan to his descendants. Abraham marked the occasion by building altars to God at Shechem and Bethel, both important religious centers in later times.

Abraham continued south to the desert area of the Negev and was forced by famine to seek refuge in Egypt. Because Abraham was fearful that the Egyptian Pharaoh would kill him in order to make Sarah one of his wives, he told her to pose as his sister. Predictably, Pharaoh took Sarah into his harem and gave Abraham presents as a sign of his gratitude. But because Pharaoh had taken another man's wife – albeit unwittingly –

God afflicted his household with serious diseases. When he realized that he had been deceived, the angry king ordered Abraham to leave the country.

Abraham returned with the wealth from Pharaoh's gifts to Bethel. There he and Lot parted company because of a shortage of suitable land for their flocks. Lot chose the fertile Jordan Valley and settled in Sodom, one of the valley cities, while Abraham stayed in Canaan. At this point, God again promised Abraham that He would give this land to his descendants, who would be as numerous as the "dust on the Earth." Abraham then moved his tents near the "great trees of Mamre" by Hebron, and built another altar to the Lord.

✡ *A rescue and a covenant* ✡

Meanwhile, in Lot's new homeland, four foreign kings and five local rulers went to war, taking Lot captive in the process. When word of the captivity reached Abraham, he gathered 318 trained men from his household and effected a rescue. Afterward, Melchizedek, a priest-king from Salem – that is, Jerusalem – brought an offering of bread and wine to Abraham and blessed him. Abraham responded by pledging him a tithe, or a tenth, of all he owned.

Some time later, the "word of the Lord" again appeared to Abraham, reassuring him that God would protect him. God also said Abraham would have a son and heir from "your own body"; that his offspring would be as numerous as the stars;

and that they would be given the land of Canaan. God solemnized His promise with a ritual sacrifice in which Abraham laid out three severed animals, placing the halves of each animal opposite of each other. After this, God told him that his descendants would be enslaved in Egypt but would escape and that he, Abraham, would die in

God promises Abraham that he will have as many offspring as there are stars in the sky, in this 19th-century painting by Julius Schnorr von Carolsfeld.

peace at a ripe old age. Then, "when the sun had set and darkness had fallen," God appeared as "a smoking firepot with a blazing torch" and passed between the pieces of the sacrificed animals. Finally, God "made a covenant," or treaty, with Abraham, telling him that his descendants would occupy the land from the Nile to the Euphrates.

✡ To Egypt and back ✡

God's call to Abraham at Haran set in motion the first events that would eventually result in the formation of the tribes of Israel and their occupation of Canaan. Genesis presents a series of snapshots that establish the major themes in Abraham's life. From the start Abraham showed remarkable obedience and faith. Called by God, he did not hesitate to set out for the unknown territory of Canaan and, once there, to build altars to mark out its future status as the Holy Land. Abraham and his household must have moved from place to place, seeking out new pastures for their animals. When famine struck, they headed for the fertile land of Egypt.

The hills of Gilead can be seen across the Jordan Valley. Abraham and his family would have become familiar with these hills during their stays in Canaan.

Some scholars believe the Egyptian episode was designed to show how Abraham gained great wealth and outwitted a figure as great as Pharaoh. Others have pointed out that his behavior toward Sarah was not honorable. Instead of trusting God to safeguard his wife, he took action to ensure his own safety. When Pharaoh rebuked him for his subterfuge, Abraham had no defense.

A caravan of camels provide modern tourists with an ancient form of travel in the Sahara. Camels are one of the animals that Abraham may have used to transport his family and belongings to Canaan.

Back in Canaan, Abraham gave Lot first choice of land. Guided by greed – not God – Lot chose land that was fertile but in the midst of hostile communities. When they went to battle, Lot was taken captive. Abraham, however, was rewarded for his unselfishness by a promise from God.

> " *'To your descendants I give this land, from the river of Egypt to the great river, the Euphrates...'* "
>
> GENESIS 15:18

After he had vanquished the four kings holding Lot prisoner, Abraham met Melchizedek, whose name means "king of righteousness." This mysterious figure appears out of nowhere. He blessed Abraham in the name of "God Most High," a title that the Canaanites applied to their supreme god and that Abraham identified with the Lord. Later, in the Christian Era, the author of the New Testament letter to the Hebrews speculated that Melchizedek, as a priest-king, foreshadowed Jesus Christ; and some Christians have identified his offerings of bread and wine with the ritual meal of the Eucharist, or Mass, which commemorates Jesus' Last Supper.

Some time later, Abraham had another vision of God and the promise that Abraham would have countless offspring – even though he and Sarah were old and childless. God confirmed His promise that Abraham's offspring would inherit Canaan with an unusual ritual similar to one retold in Jeremiah (34:18–20). On this occasion, the people of Jerusalem made a solemn oath by walking between the halves of a slaughtered calf, signifying that God should treat them like the calf if they did not keep their oath. Here, God was making an oath to Abraham. God's participation in the ritual in the form of smoke and fire – traditional manifestations of the divine presence – was evidence that God would fulfill the promise of the covenant He had made with Abraham: that his descendants would possess Canaan. ▲

MESSAGE
— *for* —
TODAY

ABRAHAM WAS A nomadic farmer when God called on him to travel to Canaan. Although Abraham was entering an unknown land full of potential danger, he never questioned God but willingly assembled his family, servants, and belongings and made the journey.

God can speak to us as well, in many ways and often at times when we least expect it. God's call may take the form of an external event that shakes us, or it may be an inner feeling that surprises us. It may urge us to follow a new path – in our career, our surroundings, or our lifestyle.

Like Abraham, we often have to take the first obedient steps in faith, without knowing where God will lead us. It is sufficient to recognize that the time has come to follow God's call and to seek our own Promised Land.

The PROMISE of a SON

ISHMAEL and ISAAC
GENESIS 16–18

> " 'I will bless her so that she will be the mother of nations;
> kings of peoples will come from her.' "
> GENESIS 17:16

ALTHOUGH THE LORD had promised Abraham that he would have a son from "his own body," to Sarah, who was now over 70 years of age, this eventuality seemed unlikely. So she suggested to Abraham that he sleep with her Egyptian maid Hagar, so that they could "build a family through her." Abraham agreed to this plan.

But in her newfound status as a mother-to-be, Hagar began to treat her mistress with disdain, provoking Sarah to retaliate with such harshness that Hagar was forced to flee Abraham's household into the desert. There, by a spring or well, "the angel of the Lord" told Hagar she must return to Sarah, assuring Hagar that her descendants would be "too numerous to count." The angel said that Hagar would have a son who would be called Ishmael and who would grow into "a wild donkey of a man" and "live in hostility toward all his brothers." Hagar realized that the angel was the Lord Himself, so she addressed Him as El Roi, the "One who sees." (Genesis mentions that the title was given to the well where they had spoken – Beer Lahai Roi.) Hagar returned home, and in due course, as God had predicted, she gave birth to Ishmael.

When Abraham was 99 years of age, God appeared to him and confirmed His covenant with the Patriarch. As Abraham fell prostrate, God told him his name would no longer be Abram ("exalted father") but Abraham ("father of many"), since his offspring would proliferate and become "many nations." In a momentous statement, God declared that His covenant with Abraham and his descendants would last forever. God would give the land of Canaan to Abraham's descendants as an "everlasting possession" and be their God. In return, as a sign of keeping the covenant, Abraham and all his male offspring must undergo the rite of circumcision – the removal of the foreskin from the penis.

✡ "Mother of nations" ✡

God also told Abraham that his wife Sarai was to be called Sarah – both names mean "princess" – and that she would be the "mother of nations." When Abraham heard that Sarah would be a mother, even though she was 90 years of age, he laughed with disbelief. But God reassured him she would have a son, whom they would call Isaac ("he laughs"). Hagar's son Ishmael would be blessed and made into "a great nation," but it would be through Isaac that God would establish His covenant. After the Lord had spoken, Abraham immediately had himself, Ishmael, and every male in his household circumcised.

Some time later, Abraham was outside his tent near "the great trees of Mamre" when he saw three men. (They were revealed to be two angels and the Lord Himself.) Abraham offered them hospitality, including a meal of curds, milk, and a "choice, tender calf." While they were eating their food, the Lord said that in a year's time Sarah

Three angels sit down *to a meal at Abraham and Sarah's table, in this
16th-century icon from the Pskov School in Russia. In Abraham's time,
it was customary for the hosts to stand by as servants to their guests.*

The PROMISE *of a* SON ▲ 17

would have a son. When Sarah overheard these words, she laughed, as Abraham had, with incredulity. The Lord heard her and told Abraham that nothing was beyond His power. Now frightened by this mysterious stranger, Sarah denied that she had laughed, but the Lord insisted that she had.

✡ Sarah and Hagar ✡

The story of Ishmael's birth and the promise of the birth of Isaac begins with Sarah longing for motherhood yet aware of its improbability because of her old age and previous barrenness. Abraham must have told Sarah that God had promised them offspring. But Sarah lacked the faith to believe that she could be their mother, so she persuaded her husband to sleep with her maid, a common custom in the ancient Middle East.

The maid's pregnancy, however, resulted in antagonism between the two women. When Abraham refused to protect Hagar from Sarah's anger, she felt compelled to flee. Hagar traveled on the "road to Shur," the main caravan route to her homeland, the Nile delta of Egypt. In the southwestern section of the Negev Desert, Hagar came to a halt near a well, doubtless exhausted and thirsty. There, Hagar met the angel who told her

God climbs down a ladder from heaven to make a covenant with the prostrate Abraham, as depicted in this 11th-century Anglo-Saxon illustration belonging to St. Augustine's Church in Canterbury, England.

about the destiny of her son Ishmael. His name, meaning "God hears," would remind her that God had responded to her suffering. Ishmael would be like a "wild donkey," that is, strong and independent. His descendants – by tradition, the Arab people – would live in proximity to the descendants of Isaac, the Israelites, but the two groups would be in constant conflict.

Some time after this visitation, in one of the most significant passages in Genesis, God confirmed the covenant he had made with Abraham in 15:18. God stressed that the relationship would be an "everlasting" one, and it would extend to Abraham's offspring. For his part, Abraham had to institute the rite of circumcision. This was, in fact, practiced by other peoples in the ancient Middle East, including the Egyptians, for whom it marked the onset of puberty. But for Abraham's descendants, circumcision had to take place on the eighth day after birth and was a sign not of manhood but of obedience and commitment to God's covenant. It was a physical symbol of the covenant and Israel's unique spiritual relationship with the Lord. Any man who was not circumcised would be "cut off from his people" and considered to have broken God's covenant (17:14).

The Genesis account moves next to the event at Mamre, where God promised that Sarah would give birth to a son, Isaac, and that through him He would continue to fulfill His promises. It is not clear whether Abraham at first recognized that the

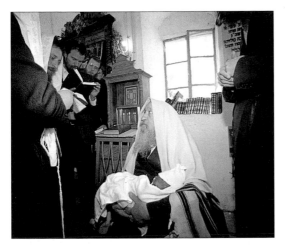

Prayers are said over a baby boy before a circumcision is performed during a modern ceremony in Israel. Jews practice circumcision to fulfill their covenant with God.

"three men" were not human. Regardless, he showed traditional Middle Eastern hospitality. He hurried to greet his guests, bowing low to the ground and calling for water to wash their dusty feet. He then arranged a meal, standing near them in the attitude of a servant while they ate.

> ❝ *'I have found favor in your eyes, my lord, do not pass your servant by.'* ❞
>
> GENESIS 18:3

The focus of the story lies at the entrance of the tent, where Sarah chuckled at the assertion that she would have a child. Her laugh of disbelief prompted the Lord to reply: "Is anything too hard for the Lord?" She, like Abraham, who laughed in a similar instance, had to learn that for the God of all creation, old age was not a barrier to giving birth. For Christians, the situation is mirrored in the New Testament when the angel Gabriel told Mary that her relative Elizabeth, "who was said to be barren," would give birth to a child, John the Baptist. On this occasion, Mary, too, was told "nothing is impossible with God [Luke 1:37]." ▲

MESSAGE
—for—
TODAY

IN THE IMPORTANT personal moments of our lives — birthdays, weddings, and anniversaries — why do we make special celebratory arrangements, often giving a gift? Whether or not we are able to say how we feel in words, our rituals become a physical way to express our feelings to those whom we care about most. This applies even more to our relationship with God, which transcends the limits of ordinary language.

For Abraham and his descendants, circumcision was an expression of belief. It was a mark of the covenant — the enduring relationship between them and God. As it was enacted by each new generation, it became a mighty vehicle for retelling the tales of God's visitation and blessing. When we reenact the rituals of religious beliefs, we, too, can celebrate our relationship with God.

CITIES of SINNERS

The DESTRUCTION of SODOM and GOMORRAH

GENESIS 18:16–19:38

*" Then the Lord said, 'The outcry against Sodom
and Gomorrah is so great and their sin so grievous...' "*

GENESIS 18:20

THE THREE MEN who had enjoyed Abraham's hospitality at Mamre walked with him to a point where they could see Sodom. One of the cities of the plain, it lay far off near the southeastern end of the Dead Sea. There Lot and his family had their home. But God had heard the "outcry against Sodom" and the neighboring Gomorrah. He intended to find out whether the outcry was justified. In light of the great destiny He had chosen for Abraham and his children, God decided to tell him what was in store.

While the two angels went to Sodom to investigate its alleged immorality, Abraham "remained standing before the Lord." He was alarmed that God might destroy the righteous among the city's inhabitants, which included his nephew Lot. So he reasoned with God. If there were 50 righteous people in the city, he said, then God surely would spare it. God agreed to his request. No doubt sensing that he was being optimistic, Abraham revised the figure of 50 downward. Eventually, God promised that if there were only 10 righteous people in Sodom, He would not destroy the city.

Meanwhile, in Sodom, Lot saw the two angels arrive in town. He pressed them to stay in his home for the night and they accepted his invitation. But late in the evening, a mob of men of all ages gathered outside Lot's house and demanded that he surrender the two strangers so that the townsmen could have sex with them. Lot went out and tried to reason with them, even offering to give them his two virgin daughters instead of his guests. But the men were incensed by Lot's resistance, and threatening to abuse him too, they "moved forward to break down the door."

The two angels took action. They dragged Lot back inside to safety, slammed the door shut, and struck the aggressors with blindness. They then urged Lot to flee with his family, informing him that God was going to destroy the city. Lot tried to warn his two prospective sons-in-law, but they thought he was joking. By this time it was dawn, and time was running out.

✡ Escaping destruction ✡

The two angels personally escorted Lot, his wife, and their two daughters from the doomed city and told them to flee to the mountains without looking back or stopping. When Lot pleaded to take refuge in the nearby town of Zoar, God consented. As soon as Lot's family was safe, God "rained down burning sulfur on Sodom and Gomorrah," destroying both the cities and the entire plain. But as the flames rose skyward, Lot's wife looked back, not heeding the angels' warning, and "became a pillar of salt." The next morning, Abraham gazed toward the cities and saw plumes of smoke rise, as if "from a furnace."

In an epilogue to the story, Lot and his two daughters moved from Zoar to a cave in the nearby mountains. There, bereft of their fiancés and isolated from other men, Lot's daughters

Lot and his daughters, led by the two angels, escape from Sodom, in this 17th-century painting by Louis de Caullery. Lot's wife was turned into a pillar of salt.

plotted to make their father drunk and sleep with him, "to preserve our family line." On successive nights, the two women achieved their purpose, with Lot apparently unaware of what was going on. Each woman gave birth to a son – Moab and Ben-Ammi. They became the ancestors, Genesis says, of the Ammonites and Moabites – hostile neighbors of the Israelites in later times.

✿ God's judgment ✿

The story of the destruction of the "cities of the plain" begins with God taking Abraham into his confidence in the manner of a friend. In turn, Abraham tried to intercede on behalf of the righteous citizens of Sodom. For Abraham, it was inconceivable that God, "the Judge of all the Earth," would kill the righteous along with the sinners. He must have been reassured at God's willingness to save Sodom for the sake of only 10 righteous people. But, as the story implies, those 10 people were not to be found.

Sodom, as recorded in the Bible, was notorious for its unfriendliness and pride. The prophet Ezekiel wrote of the citizens being "arrogant, overfed, and unconcerned" toward the "poor and needy [16:49]." In the New Testament, Jesus

referred to Sodom (Matthew 10:15) when he warned of the fate of the towns that rejected him.

With the arrival of the two angels, Lot insisted that they stay with him, because he knew the dangers they would face from the other citizens. Lot's fears materialized in the form of a depraved mob. His attempt to appease them by offering his daughters may seem unthinkable. In accordance with the customs of his time, however, Lot may have seen responsibility as a host to protect his guests as his top priority.

> **❝ *Then the Lord rained down burning sulfur on Sodom and Gomorrah…* ❞**
> GENESIS 19:24

The angels, who had been protected by Lot, now protected him, using their supernatural power to blind the culprits. But even with the evidence of their miracle-working, Lot hesitated to leave the city. Perhaps he had second thoughts after his sons-in-law's reaction,

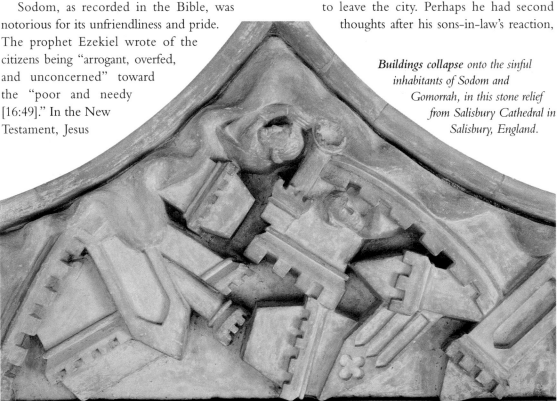

Buildings collapse onto the sinful inhabitants of Sodom and Gomorrah, in this stone relief from Salisbury Cathedral in Salisbury, England.

Salt formations in the Dead Sea, Israel, are reminiscent of the form Lot's wife might have taken when she failed to heed the angels' warning not to look back at Sodom.

MESSAGE
— for —
TODAY

THE STORY OF *the infamy of Sodom and Gomorrah represents all that can go wrong in a society. What was remarkable about Abraham was his reluctance to abandon all the inhabitants to their fate as long as it meant also condemning the innocents in the city. In a similar way, we should not condemn all the citizens of a country because we disagree with the actions of its government.*

Abraham cared so much about Lot and any other "righteous" Sodomites that he was even willing to stand up to God and argue his case. His bargaining session with God can be seen as one of the first prayers in the Bible. It shows that an individual can have a two-way relationship with God. While acknowledging God's awesome power, we understand that God hears our heartfelt requests.

or he felt too attached to his home and possessions. Whatever the reason, the angels had to forcibly lead him and his family to safety.

Scholars have speculated that the actual destruction of Sodom and the other cities may have been caused by an earthquake – the cities were located in a seismic zone – which may have ignited the natural reserves of bitumen, petroleum, and sulfur found in the area. But Genesis stresses that the destruction was a result of divine judgment. The fate of Lot's wife warns of the consequences of disobeying a divine warning. Indeed, Jesus Christ uttered a warning in connection with his Second Coming, the time when he would return to usher in a new world order. He said, "no one in the field should go back… Remember Lot's wife! Whoever tries to keep his life will lose it, and whoever loses his life will preserve it [Luke 17:31–33]."

After the destruction, the focus switches to Abraham, as he surveys the ruins. After the maelstrom of fire and brimstone, Genesis reminds its readers of the relationship between Abraham and God, stating that God honored Abraham's intercession when He brought Lot out of catastrophe. ▲

RESCUED *from the* DESERT

The DISMISSAL *of* HAGAR
GENESIS 21:1–21

> *Then she went off and sat down nearby, about a bow-shot away, for she thought, 'I cannot watch the boy die.'*
>
> GENESIS 21:16

ONE YEAR AFTER God's incredible promise to Abraham that his wife would have a child (Genesis 17:19), Sarah gave birth to a son. They named him Isaac, as God had instructed. Eight days later, the boy was circumcised, in accordance with God's covenant (Genesis 17:10).

Isaac's next rite of passage came two or three years later, when he was weaned from his mother, and Abraham celebrated the event with a feast. During the festivities, Sarah caught Ishmael, Abraham's son by her servant Hagar, "mocking" Isaac, and she flew into a rage. She ordered Abraham to throw both son and mother out of his household, exclaiming that Ishmael would "never share in the inheritance with my son Isaac."

When Hagar was cast out previously (Genesis 16:6), Abraham had seemed indifferent. He was distressed at this new demand. God, however, told him to obey Sarah, reassuring him that both sons would have many children. But it would be through Isaac, God said, that Abraham's "offspring will be reckoned" – Isaac would inherit the covenant. So Abraham provided food and water for Hagar and Ishmael, and sent the two away to wander in the desert of Beersheba.

Eventually, exhausted and out of water, Hagar placed Ishmael under a bush. She was convinced that her son had not long to live, and not wanting to see him die, she walked a short distance away. She then sat down and began to sob. But God heard Ishmael crying and comforted Hagar,

The forsaken Ishmael and Hagar are depicted in the desert, in this 19th-century French painting by Jean-Charles Cazin. When God heard the boy cry, He opened Hagar's eyes, and her gaze fell on a well of water.

telling her not to be afraid and to go to her son, whom He would make into "a great nation." He "opened her eyes, and she saw a well of water."

Ishmael grew up in the desert with God's protection and became an archer. Later on, at a time when he was living in the desert of Paran in north-central Sinai, his mother arranged his marriage to a woman from Egypt, her home country.

✡ An occasion for laughter ✡

The birth of Isaac was the most tangible fulfillment of God's promise to Abraham up to this point. When he was born, Sarah joyfully said, "God has brought me laughter, and everyone who hears about this will laugh with me."

Despite her joy in giving birth, however, Sarah soon worried that Ishmael represented a threat to Isaac's inheritance. In a patriarchal world, domestic situations involving the sons of more than one mother often led to intense rivalry. In later times, laws would establish the rules of inheritance. According to Deuteronomy 21:17, the eldest son received a double share of the inheritance, and unless there were no sons, daughters inherited nothing. Neither did the sons of female slaves or servants receive an inheritance, unless they were legally adopted by their father. Abraham might have adopted Ishmael, which would explain Sarah's vehemence in wanting to get rid of him.

Even though Ishmael's departure was prompted by jealousy, it was apparently part of God's providential plan that Abraham's two sons should be separated and become the progenitors of neighboring but antagonistic peoples. While Ishmael would father a great nation, it was through Isaac that God's covenant would be fulfilled. In the New Testament, Paul developed this fundamental difference between the two sons. Writing to the Galatians, Paul compared Ishmael, the son of "the slave woman," to the Jews, whom he believed were slaves to the Jewish Law. Isaac, the son of the "free woman," he compared to Christians, the free "children of the promise [Galatians 4:21–33]." ▲

MESSAGE — for — TODAY

THIS EPISODE SEEMS to be cruel and unjust. Because Isaac is preferred over his brother Ishmael, both Ishmael and his mother are sent away into the desert. One of the strengths of the Bible is its truthfulness. It does not present a rosy picture of life, but illustrates realities – including family tensions and questionable, even wrong, decisions.

It is possible to speculate that Abraham and Sarah set the stage for this family tragedy when they decided that Abraham should sleep with Hagar, thus demonstrating their lack of faith in God's promise. The result has been thousands of years of enmity between two related nations. Perhaps it is a reminder to take God at His word and wait patiently in faith. To do otherwise may mean sacrificing the best that God has in store for us.

The ULTIMATE TEST

The BINDING of ISAAC
GENESIS 22:1–19

> " *Then God said, 'Take your son, your only son, Isaac, whom you love, and go to the region of Moriah. Sacrifice him there as a burnt offering on one of the mountains I will tell you about.'* "
> GENESIS 22:2

SOME YEARS AFTER he had dismissed Hagar and Ishmael from his household, Abraham was faced with the ultimate trial of his faith in God. Abraham and Sarah's only, beloved son Isaac had grown to be an adolescent. Without providing any reasons, Genesis relates that God ordered Abraham to take Isaac to one of the mountains in the region of Moriah and sacrifice the youth as a burnt offering.

Without hesitating, Abraham faithfully obeyed God's instructions. He rose early the next morning, saddled his donkey, and took with him Isaac and two of his servants. Abraham then chopped enough wood for the sacrifice, and the group set off from Beersheba.

After traveling for three days, Abraham spotted the mountain where God had told him to go. Concealing his true purpose, he ordered his servants to stay with the donkey while he and Isaac went on to the designated spot to worship. Giving Isaac the bundle of wood to carry, Abraham took the "fire and the knife," and together they continued their journey.

Isaac recognized the materials they were bringing with them as those that were typically used to perform a sacrifice. So Isaac asked his father, "The fire and wood are here…but where is the lamb for the burnt offering?" Abraham assured his son that God would provide the lamb, and they continued walking.

When they finally reached the place of the impending sacrifice, Abraham built an altar and stacked the wood on it. Next, he bound Isaac, placed him on top of the wood, and picked up the knife to kill him. Only at that critical moment did one of God's angels call out to Abraham from heaven, telling him not to touch the boy. Abraham had shown his faith in God through his willingness to sacrifice his own son. God did not intend that the deed be done.

✡ A renewed blessing ✡

After the angel had spoken, Abraham looked up and saw a ram caught by its horns in a nearby thicket. So he went over to the animal, disentangled it, and killed and burned it as an offering in Isaac's place.

Afterward, the angel spoke to the Patriarch once again. Because Abraham had not withheld his son from the sacrifice, the angel said, God would bless him and make his offspring "as numerous as the stars in the sky and as the sand on the seashore." Furthermore, his descendants would conquer their enemies' cities, and through the children of Abraham, "all nations on Earth would be blessed." All this would happen, the

angel reiterated, because Abraham had unquestionably obeyed the word of God. When the angel had finished speaking, Abraham and Isaac rejoined the two servants, and the group set off back to Beersheba.

✡ A faithful sacrifice ✡

The test of Abraham's faith is depicted in this 13th-century Danish manuscript illustration. As Abraham poises to slay Isaac, one of God's angels stops him and praises his obedience. A ram in the thicket, evidently supplied by God, is sacrificed for the burnt offering.

The understated account of Abraham binding Isaac for a sacrifice is one of the best-known stories in the Bible. This episode represents the climax of Abraham's faith in God. In what appears to be an affront to both reason and compassion, Abraham was ordered to sacrifice his only son. He no longer had Ishmael, his son by Hagar. Now he must kill his one remaining child and heir. Yet he must have recalled God's words that it would be through Isaac that "your offspring will be reckoned [Genesis 21:12]." How could God reconcile that promise with a command to sacrifice Isaac? While Abraham's inward reaction to God is not stated, the choice between killing his son and obeying God must have nearly broken his heart. His prompt departure for the mountain, however, indicates his resolve to obey the command of God.

pronoun "we" may suggest that despite the horrendous deed he was commanded to perform, Abraham still hoped that God would somehow allow him and his son to return together.

> ❝ *Abraham looked up and there in a thicket he saw a ram caught by its horns.* ❞
> GENESIS 22:13

Abraham's faith must have been at breaking point when he raised the knife to cut Isaac's throat. At this moment of conclusive, demonstrated faith, God stopped the sacrifice. As Abraham had earlier indicated to Isaac, although he may not have known the truth of his words, the Lord provided a sacrificial animal – a ram caught in a bush. Then God swore an oath in His own name – the only time in Genesis – and rewarded Abraham by restating and adding to His promise. Abraham's descendants would not only inherit Canaan but conquer it by force, and they would proliferate throughout the Earth and cause the rest of the world to be blessed.

✡ *The traditional offering* ✡

The story sheds light on the practice of sacrifice in the world of the Patriarchs. According to the Bible, those who worshiped God offered sacrifices from the earliest times. In Genesis 4:4, for example, Abel offered God the "fat portions from some of the firstborn of his flock." And Isaac's question to his father about the lamb shows that he was familiar with the rite.

The reasons for performing a sacrifice could vary. Some sacrifices were carried out to give thanks to God. Others accompanied a vow or were intended to expiate sin. Sacrificial offerings could include bread and oil or animals that were burnt whole. It was thought that the blood of an animal was its life and so could save people from the consequence of their sins (Leviticus 17:11).

Abraham leads Isaac *toward the sacrificial site on the mountain, in this 15th-century painting by a Hungarian artist. Isaac carries the wood for the burnt offering.*

The site of the ritual on a mountain in the region of Moriah was later identified as the hill in Jerusalem on which the temple was built by Solomon (2 Chronicles 3:1). This location is now crowned with the Muslim shrine known as the Dome of the Rock. When Abraham and his party arrived there, he told his servants to wait until "we will come back to you." The use of the

Some scholars have speculated that the story in Genesis may refer to a time when the Israelites performed child sacrifice, which was later prohibited by Israelite law on penalty of death (Leviticus 18:21; 20:2). Certainly, the practice was known to have occurred in the ancient Middle East; for example, among the people of Canaan, the land that Abraham was called to by God. So the story might be partly "etiological"; that is, intended to account for something's origin – in this case, how animals were substituted for children in sacrifices.

✡ Parallel stories ✡

The episode, with its idea of a sacrificial victim and its theme of substitution, has attracted generations of Christian readers. Many of them have thought that it foreshadows the sacrificial death of Jesus Christ. Abraham gave up his only son Isaac to be sacrificed, just as God, according to Christian belief, gave up His only son Jesus. The image of Isaac carrying the bundle of wood to the sacrificial spot is paralleled by Jesus carrying his cross on the way to Golgotha, the place of his crucifixion. The references to the sacrificial lamb are a reminder that Jesus was known as "the lamb of God [John 1:29]." And the way that Isaac seems to yield willingly to Abraham is mirrored by Jesus allowing himself to be sacrificed on the cross on behalf of the sinners of the world. ▲

This Syrian stone figure, from the 18th century BC, is holding a ram ready for a sacrifice. In Abraham's time, the rite of sacrificing an animal as a burnt offering was a common practice. The animal was usually a ram, young bull, or male goat.

MESSAGE
—for—
TODAY

WHEN GOD instructed Abraham to sacrifice his son Isaac, "whom you love," not only did Abraham face the loss of his beloved son, but also the promise that he would become the father of a great nation. That great dream seemed about to disappear. Yet Abraham was willing to give up both his present and his future because he trusted God.

Crises arise in our lives, and sometimes they sorely test our faith. It can appear that doing God's will may cause us great loss, even of what God has promised. For instance, we may find that moral action puts our job at risk; yet God promises to provide what we need. Remembering God's timely provision for faithful Abraham can give us added energy and faith to do what is right, and to trust the outcome to God.

SARAH'S DEATH

The TOMB of the PATRIARCHS
GENESIS 23

"'Sell me some property for a burial site here so that I can bury my dead.'"
GENESIS 23:4

AFTER ABRAHAM HAD proved his faith by his willingness to sacrifice Isaac, he and his family continued to live in Beersheba. At some point, however, they moved to Hebron, about 20 miles (30 km) to the north. There, Sarah, Abraham's wife, died at an impressive 127 years of age.

Abraham was filled with grief at the loss of Sarah and wept over her lifeless body. When he had recovered, he decided to secure a proper burial place for her. So he went to the main gate of Hebron and there spoke to some of the Hittite people (pp. 88–89). The Hittites acknowledged Abraham as a "mighty prince" and told him he could bury his dead in one of their tombs. But Abraham had set his heart on another burial site – the "cave of Machpelah," which lay at the end of a field belonging to a Hittite named Ephron.

When Ephron heard Abraham's request, he offered to give the Patriarch the cave and the field

The burial place for Sarah, in the cave of Machpelah, is surrounded by walls from the time of Herod the Great. Her grave is under a building that is now a mosque.

in which it was situated. Bowing down before the Hittite group in a gesture of courtesy, Abraham insisted on paying "the price of the field." Without directly accepting his offer, Ephron mentioned that the field was worth 400 shekels of silver. Abraham agreed to pay this price and took possession of the property. After the transaction had been completed, in the presence of witnesses, Abraham buried Sarah in the cave.

✡ A burial in Canaan ✡

The death of Sarah marks the end of the first significant woman to appear in the stories of the Patriarchs. Sarah's life was not easy. She was deprived of children until she was 90 years of age. She suffered the experience of Pharaoh's harem. And her relationship with her maidservant Hagar was the source of much pain and conflict.

Genesis emphasizes how much grief Abraham suffered at the loss of his loyal wife. At the same time, it stresses Abraham's determination to become the legal owner of a tomb not only for Sarah but also for other family members, including himself (Genesis 25:9).

The Hittites offered Abraham "the choicest of their tombs," but he wanted one that was distinct from those of other people. It may seem odd that Ephron offered to give him the field for nothing. According to Hittite records, however, a landowner was obliged to fulfill certain financial and social obligations. If a landowner sold part of a plot, he still had to pay dues for the entire property. Ephron may have wanted to give Abraham the whole field to escape obligations that went with it. In any case, Abraham insisted on paying 400 shekels, an exorbitant price compared with the 17 shekels the prophet Jeremiah paid for a field (Jeremiah 32:9) or the 20 shekels the Midianites paid for Joseph (pp. 64–67). Yet it meant that Abraham owned a piece of Canaan, the land that God had promised to him and his descendants (Genesis 12:7). In buying it, Abraham confirmed his commitment to God's promise. ▲

MESSAGE
— for —
TODAY

AS SOMEONE WHO spent the majority of his life looking with longing toward the fulfillment of God's promises, Abraham particularly desired to have a piece of the Promised Land that he could call his own. He chose the field of Machpelah — now known as Hebron — and it became the family burial plot.

The ability to say "this land is my land" has resonated throughout history ever since. Having a place that we can call home signifies that we have roots and common ground with our relatives. In today's world, when family members typically move far apart, claiming common spiritual ground by faith has become all the more significant. When we trust God, we know that we claim God's promises for an inheritance full of love and blessing.

A WIFE for ISAAC

ISAAC and REBEKAH
GENESIS 24

> " *'I want you to swear by the Lord…that you will not get a wife*
> *for my son from the daughters of the Canaanites.'* "
>
> GENESIS 24:3

WHEN ABRAHAM WAS "well advanced in years," he decided that it was time for his son Isaac to be married. So he asked his chief servant to swear that he would find a wife for him. The servant was not to look in Canaan, where they were living, however. Instead, he was to find Isaac's bride from among Abraham's relatives in Haran, northern Mesopotamia, where he had originally been called by God.

The servant asked Abraham whether he should take Isaac to Mesopotamia if the woman he chose did not want to leave home. Abraham replied firmly that Isaac should stay in Canaan. He assured the servant that an angel of God would guide him; if he could not find a suitable woman, he would be released from his oath.

The servant swore the oath to Abraham and departed with 10 camels and "all kinds of good things." He traveled to the district of Haran and the "town of Nahor." This may refer to the town where Abraham's brother Nahor lived or to a town of the same name that is known to have existed near Haran.

When the servant eventually reached his destination, it was late in the day. Remaining outside the town walls, he took his camels near a well of water and prayed to the "God of my master Abraham" for success. As he watched the women of the town coming out to fetch water in the cool of evening, he asked God for a sign: "May it be that when I say to a girl, 'Please let down your jar that I may have a drink,' and she says, 'Drink, and I'll water your camels too' – let her be the one you have chosen for your servant Isaac."

At that moment, a "very beautiful" girl named Rebekah, who was the granddaughter of Abraham's brother Nahor, came to the well with her jar. The servant saw her, rushed up, and asked her for water. Not only did she give him water but also "drew enough for all his camels." The servant studied her closely, wondering whether she could really be the right girl. When she had finished watering the camels, he gave her gifts of a gold nose ring and bracelets. Then he asked her who she was and whether he could stay the night in her father's house. She told him she was the daughter of Bethuel, the son of Nahor and Milcah, and assured him he could stay with them. Realizing that he was among Abraham's relatives, the servant bowed down and praised God.

✡ A marriage agreed ✡

Meanwhile, Rebekah returned home to give her account of what had just happened. As soon as her brother Laban saw the ring and bracelets she was wearing, he hurried to the well. Greeting the servant with the words "Come, you who are blessed by the Lord," he welcomed the servant into their house.

The servant accepted his offer of hospitality and went home with Laban. Before eating the food set before him, however, the servant insisted

on describing how he came to be at Nahor. He spoke of the oath he had made to Abraham, his prayer at the well, and how Rebekah's response to his request for water had been the sign he was looking for. When they heard his story, Laban and Bethuel realized "this is from the Lord," and told the servant he could take Rebekah back to Canaan. With his mission completed, the servant "bowed down to the ground before the Lord," then presented gold and silver jewelry and other gifts to Rebekah, her brother, and her mother.

Although Laban and Rebekah's mother wanted Rebekah to stay with them for another 10 days, Abraham's servant insisted on leaving for Canaan the next morning. After receiving her family's blessing, Rebekah and her maids prepared

Abraham's servant chooses Rebekah as Isaac's wife, in this 17th-century French painting by Nicolas Poussin. Abraham wished Isaac to marry someone from his native land, not a pagan Canaanite woman.

for the journey. Then she mounted her camel and set off for a new life.

At this point the story returns to Isaac. Genesis implies that during the servant's absence Abraham had died: chapter 25 says he passed away when he was 175 years old and was buried in the cave of Machpelah. Isaac was now head of the clan and living in the Negev. One evening, as he was standing in his field, he saw camels approaching, bearing Rebekah, the servant, and the rest of their party. When they arrived, Isaac listened to the servant's story of what had happened. Then he welcomed Rebekah into the tent of Sarah, his late mother. "So," Genesis says, "she became his wife, and he loved her."

✿ Laban and Rebekah ✿

The successful search to find a wife for Isaac is one of the longest and most charming episodes in Genesis. The aged Abraham must have been aware that his own death was imminent, and he took steps to secure God's promise that his descendants would be as numerous "as the stars in the sky [Genesis 22:17]." He stressed, however, that his son's prospective wife should not be from among "the daughters of Canaanites" but a member of Abraham's own kin. Perhaps Abraham feared the influence of a pagan wife on his son – a fear expressed elsewhere in the Bible (1 Kings 11:1–4; Deuteronomy 7:3–4).

The person Abraham asked to perform this crucial mission was his chief servant. Traditionally identified as Eliezer of Damascus, he was so trusted that before Abraham's sons were born the Patriarch was prepared to bequeath his estate to

A gold necklace from northwestern Syria, dating from the 18th century BC, is representative of the jewelry given to Rebekah. Other gifts that might have been offered to a bride-to-be included nose rings, bracelets, and clothes.

this man (Genesis 15:2). The servant is depicted as a simple, pious soul, loyal to his master. At first he had misgivings about his task, but with Abraham's assurances, he took the oath, which meant placing his hand beneath Abraham's thigh – an act that made the oath particularly solemn.

When he reached Nahor, the servant saw that he would have to depend on God for a sign. His prayer, addressed to the Lord as "God of my master Abraham," may suggest that he did not share belief in Abraham's God. But the wording emphasizes the covenantal relationship between God and Abraham to which he, as part of Abraham's household, was also committed by circumcision (pp. 16–19).

> **❝ Before he had finished praying, Rebekah came out with her jar on her shoulder. ❞**
> GENESIS 24:15

The episode also sheds light on Laban and Rebekah, characters who feature prominently in the life of Jacob, Isaac's son. Laban is presented as a generous host and a caring brother, concerned for his sister's welfare. Some scholars, however, have suggested that his warm hospitality was influenced by the gift of the ring and bracelet to his sister. Genesis may be hinting at the grasping

A modern-day Bedouin woman covers her face with a veil, a garment worn by such women as Rebekah since Old Testament times. It is worn for modesty – only a woman's husband is permitted to look upon her face.

and scheming side of his character, which is later shown in his dealings with Jacob (pp. 44–51).

Rebekah comes across as an impulsive, generous person, showing none of the deviousness she later displayed when she tricked her elder son Esau out of his father's blessing (pp. 38–41). She unhesitatingly responded to the servant's request for water, demonstrated concern for his camels, and quickly offered hospitality to him. She willingly left for Canaan without delay.

The blessing that Rebekah received from her family as she departed – "Our sister, may you increase to thousands upon thousands" – recalls the Lord's promise given to Abraham on Mount Moriah (Genesis 22:17). It also establishes her role in the divine destiny of Israel. ▲

MESSAGE
—for—
TODAY

ABRAHAM WAS CONCERNED that Isaac should not marry a local girl. Abraham wished to safeguard the religious revolution God had instituted through him, and he knew that if Isaac joined himself to a neighboring pagan tribe, he might be tempted to follow its ways. Isaac was not expected or encouraged to "fall in love" as the means of discovering his mate. Abraham had larger concerns.

The biblical wording is significant: Isaac married Rebekah and then he loved her. Unlike in the Western world today, in which love leads to marriage, in Abraham's time it was the reverse – love grew out of the marriage. It reminds us that a successful marriage depends on the commitment and effort partners put into it. As the medieval Rabbi Yosef said, "It's only when you've lived with a person and come to know them well that you can truly say you love them."

THE STORY OF JACOB

STRUGGLING *with* GOD

GENESIS 25–35

> " *'All peoples on Earth will be blessed through you and your offspring.'* "
>
> GENESIS 28:14

BORN THE SECOND SON of Isaac and Rebekah only moments after his twin brother Esau, Jacob was destined to carry on the covenant legacy handed down by his grandfather Abraham. Genesis gives its accounts of Jacob as the third great Patriarch of Israel. The Lord renamed him Israel ("he struggles with God"), and the new name distinguished him as the forefather of the people of Israel: his 12 sons founded the 12 tribes of Israel. Through them God implemented the promises of the covenant: that Abraham and his descendants would become a great nation and possess the land of Canaan.

Jacob's story, like Abraham's, is filled with divine revelations and encounters, including visions of heaven and visitations from God. At a more human level, the story charts Jacob's spiritual pilgrimage, without shrinking from his defects or denying his virtues. Although treacherous and greedy toward Esau, he exhibits sincere remorse and piety

Jacob is portrayed in his senior years, in this detail from a 14th-century Italian fresco by Simone Martini. He lived until he was at least 147 years old.

before God. At times Jacob is depicted as being cool and calculating; at other times, he responds with spontaneity and emotion – such as when he first meets his future wife Rachel.

✡ God's providential plan ✡

Jacob's eclipse of Esau was predicted by God to Rebekah before she gave birth to her sons. Jacob ruthlessly tricked Esau out of both his birthright and – with Rebekah's assistance – his paternal blessing from Isaac. Afterward, fearing Esau's wrath, Jacob fled to his uncle Laban in Paddan Aram, a region in northern Mesopotamia.

Tricked in turn by his uncle, Jacob entered a period of servitude and married his two cousins, Leah and Rachel. He eventually escaped from his uncle and headed back toward Canaan. When Laban chased him down, the two men finally promised to respect each other's territorial boundaries. After meeting and reconciling with Esau on the road home, Jacob arrived safely back in Canaan – just as God had promised.

Despite his failings, Jacob was peculiarly blessed with several divine encounters. Each revelation from God and His angels (for example, when Jacob was visited by them at Bethel) occurred at a significant turning point in Jacob's life. On each occasion, God encouraged Jacob and confirmed his inheritance of the covenant promises.

When, in later times, the people of Israel looked back to their ancestor, they found a person flawed in character. Through his own persistence and God's guidance and blessing, Jacob was transformed into a faithful follower of God. This theme of redemption is central to Jacob's story: that God fulfills His promise not because of goodness but through His grace and guidance. ▲

Jacob fled from his brother's anger to his uncle's treachery at Haran, probably using the route traveled by traders. After 20 years, Jacob – with his two wives, children, and animals – returned to Canaan.

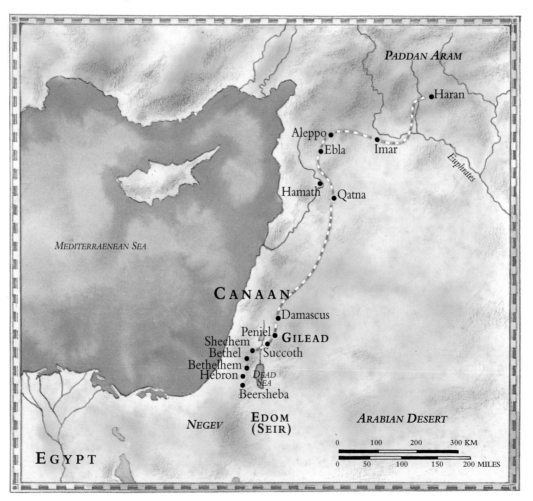

BROTHERS DIVIDED

JACOB and ESAU

GENESIS 25:19–34; 26:34–28:9

*" Esau became a skillful hunter, a man of the open country,
while Jacob was a quiet man, staying among the tents. "*
GENESIS 25:27

THE RIVALRY BETWEEN Jacob and Esau, the twin sons of Isaac and Rebekah, began before they were born. According to Genesis, Isaac prayed to God for children because Rebekah was barren, and the Lord granted his request. However, Rebekah's pregnancy was so painful that she asked God what was happening to her. He replied that that there were "two nations" in her womb. God also predicted that "one people will be stronger than the other, and the older will serve the younger."

Rebekah eventually gave birth to the twins. The first boy to emerge was red, and his body was "like a hairy garment." They called him Esau (which is similar in sound to the Hebrew for "hairy") and also Edom ("red"). The second boy was born clinging to his brother's heel and was named Jacob ("he grasps the heel" or "he deceives"). As the boys grew up, Esau became a skilled hunter and was Isaac's favorite because he could satisfy his father's appetite for "wild game." Rebekah, however, preferred Jacob, a quiet person who liked to stay at home.

One day Esau returned home ravenous from a hard day's hunting. When he saw Jacob cooking a delicious "red stew" of lentils, he implored his brother to give him some. But Jacob, taking advantage of Esau's hunger, demanded as payment his older brother's birthright – Esau's rights of inheritance as the eldest son. In the grip of his terrible hunger, feeling that he was about to die,

Esau agreed to the deal, and as Jacob demanded, confirmed it with an oath. "So," Genesis states, "Esau despised his birthright."

✡ Blessing the wrong son ✡

Years later, when Isaac was old, blind, and frail and thought he would not live much longer, he told Esau to hunt and cook some wild game for him, after which he would bless his son. However, Rebekah overheard Isaac's words and plotted to procure Isaac's blessing for Jacob. She made a stew from two goats. Then she dressed Jacob in Esau's clothes, covering his hands and his neck with goatskins to imitate Esau's hairiness.

Jacob, in disguise, brought the stew to his father. Fooled by the "hairy" hands and the smell of the clothes, Isaac mistook the younger son for Esau and blessed him. He prayed that God would give his son an "abundance of grain and new wine" and make him "lord over your brothers." When Esau returned, bringing the requested food, Isaac was enraged to discover that he had been tricked. The distraught Esau begged Isaac for a blessing, but the first blessing, with its promise of inheritance, was irrevocable. When Esau persisted, Isaac told him that he would "live by the sword" and serve his brother, "but when you grow restless, you will throw his yoke from off your neck."

Smoldering with hatred over Jacob's treachery, Esau plotted to kill him after Isaac's death. But Rebekah heard about Esau's intentions and

Esau sells his birthright to Jacob, in this 18th-century Spanish painting by
Zacarias Gonzalez Velazquez. By doing so, Esau forfeited the covenant God
made with Abraham, which should have been passed to him as the eldest son.

As a skilled hunter using "quiver and bow," Esau would have hunted gazelles (among other animals, p. 90), as depicted in this 700 BC Mesopotamian relief.

warned Jacob to flee to her brother Laban in Haran in Mesopotamia. Not only would Jacob be safe, but he could also marry one of Laban's daughters, instead of, like Esau, a local pagan girl. Rebekah convinced Isaac of the wisdom of the marriage arrangement, then obtained a blessing for Jacob before he left.

✡ *Rights of the firstborn* ✡

The conflict between Jacob and Esau foreshadows the later rivalry between the Israelites and the Edomites, whose forefather was said to be Esau. More to the point, it shows how God could overturn social conventions – here the rights of the firstborn – for His providential plan. Indeed, the theme of the younger son displacing his brother with God's approval occurs elsewhere in the Bible, for example with Isaac and Ishmael.

In normal circumstances, the eldest son in a family enjoyed precedence over his brothers. He was given a double share of the inheritance and became head of the family upon his father's death. The firstborn could forfeit his preferential status, however, by committing a serious crime – as Jacob's son Reuben later would when he slept with his father's concubine (Genesis 35:22).

> ❝ *He did not recognize him, for his hands were hairy like those of his brother Esau…* ❞
>
> GENESIS 27:23

Inscribed tablets found at the Mesopotamian site of Nuzi reveal that the transfer of the birthright between brothers did occur in the ancient Middle East. Esau lost his birthright and blessing through his brother's deceit; yet Genesis emphasizes that Esau was too ready to forgo his birthright for a mere meal. Soon after this incident, Esau married two pagan Hittite women, who were a "source of grief to Isaac and Rebekah." In short, his actions show he cared more for transient pleasure and gratification than for establishing the discipline, religious practice, and social values that would have made him a worthy successor to his grandfather Abraham.

The stew that tempted the hungry Esau was probably made over an open fire in a cooking pot similar to this 7th-century BC clay pot and scooped out with bread.

While Jacob used questionable methods to obtain the birthright, he clearly recognized its value. Genesis stresses the importance of a deathbed blessing – it was tantamount to a prophetic declaration of a person's destiny. This is why Rebekah, knowing that Isaac intended to bless Esau, wanted her favorite, Jacob, to receive the blessing.

The episode shows dishonorable characters, and the outcome leaves each of them bitter, sad, or fearful. Jacob betrayed his brother and father. Rebekah betrayed Esau and her husband. Isaac, contrary to God's pronouncement that "the older will serve the younger," and against the convention that a dying man bless all his sons, tried to bless only his firstborn.

Yet despite the failings of these people, Genesis shows that God's plan for Abraham and his descendants continued. In the end, Jacob had to depart to Haran, where he would find a wife and provide a link in the fulfillment of God's promise to Abraham. Indeed, Isaac reiterated the promise when blessing Jacob before his departure: "May God Almighty…give you and your descendants the blessing given to Abraham, so that you may take possession of the land where you now live as an alien, the land God gave to Abraham." ▲

MESSAGE
—*for*—
TODAY

THE PROBLEMS THAT ARISE when parents choose favorite children are reflected in the story of Jacob and Esau – that their parents began to identify with them rather than each other only multiplied the problems. It is fascinating to note the measure-for-measure consequences of their choices. Rebekah took advantage of Isaac's blindness; as a result, her favorite son had to leave home. Jacob cheated his father; when he played favorites with his own sons, they deceived him, too (pp. 64–67). The lesson? All humans face the consequences of their actions over the course of time.

While the Bible acknowledges such failings, it does not justify them, but makes clear what will result from injustice, greed, and covetousness. God's grace does not depend on our goodness, but His blessings abound when we live and love His way.

A STAIRWAY to HEAVEN

JACOB'S LADDER
GENESIS 28:10–22

> **"** *'How awesome is this place! This is none other than the house of God; this is the gate of heaven.'* **"**
> GENESIS 28:17

FOLLOWING HIS MOTHER'S advice to take refuge from his angry brother, Jacob left his family home at Beersheba. He set off on the journey north to Haran in Mesopotamia. There he hoped to stay with his uncle Laban and find a wife for himself from among his extended family.

At some stage along the way, Jacob lay down to sleep after night had fallen, using a nearby stone as a pillow. As he slept, he had a powerful dream in which he saw a "stairway" joining Earth to heaven, with angels ascending and descending it. The Lord appeared to Jacob and revealed Himself as the God of Abraham and Isaac, who would give to Jacob and his descendants the land he was sleeping on – Canaan. Jacob's offspring, God declared, would be as numerous as the "dust of the Earth." They would spread around the world and, through them, everyone would

be blessed. God also assured Jacob that He would watch over him wherever he went, returning him in time to Canaan, the Promised Land. Not until He had fulfilled His promise to Jacob, God said, would He leave him.

When Jacob awoke from his sleep, he sensed the divine presence of the Lord surrounding him. Struck with awe, he proclaimed that the place must be the house of God and the entrance to heaven. Early the following day, Jacob raised up his stone "pillow" as a pillar, consecrated it by pouring oil on top of it, and named the place Bethel, which translated means as the "house of God." Jacob then vowed that if God cared for him and brought him

Jacob dreams of a ladder leading to heaven, in this 12th-century illustration from the Lambeth Bible *in England. In Jacob's dream, God revealed that He would give the land that Jacob lay upon to him and his descendants.*

home safely, then "the Lord will be my God," the stone pillar would be "God's house," and he would give God a tithe, or a tenth, of all that he owned.

✡ Sacred Bethel ✡

Genesis's account of Jacob's dream explains how Bethel became a significant Israelite sanctuary. Such was its prestige in later years that the Ark of the Covenant, which housed the tablets inscribed with the Law, was first kept there (Judges 20:27); and in the time of the prophet Amos in 750 BC, it was a place of pilgrimage.

Like many sites frequented by the Patriarchs, Bethel began as a Canaanite shrine, known as Luz. The Canaanite association was preserved in the name Bethel, literally the "house of El." El was the supreme God of the Canaanites, identified by the Israelites with the Lord. Bethel and other ancient holy sites are referred to in the Bible as *bamot* – a Hebrew word translated as "high places" – and were often marked by sacred standing stones. Jacob's raising and consecration of his "pillow" follows this tradition.

At the center of the story lies Jacob's spiritual development; it is the first recorded occasion on which he received a divine revelation. While Jacob watched the "stairway" – a word traditionally translated as ladder – linking Earth to heaven, God appeared and reaffirmed the covenant He had made with Abraham. Jacob reacted to this revelation by vowing that the Lord would be his God if He gave him "food to eat and clothes to wear" and safe conduct to and from Haran. Some scholars have criticized Jacob for his apparent inability to accept God unconditionally. Others have pointed out that Jacob responded as best he could at this stage of his life. That the beginnings of true religious feelings were woken inside him is shown by his raising and anointing the pillar, naming the site, and promising to give God a tenth of all he had. Furthermore, he acknowledged that the God of his father and grandfather could also be his own. ▲

MESSAGE —for— TODAY

WHEN JACOB LEFT his father's household, intending to travel a great distance, he thought that he had left behind his father's God. After all, he had deceived his father and tricked his brother. Jacob must have felt the rejection some individuals feel today when they believe that their own wrong actions have left them abandoned or unloved. Like Jacob, however, they may discover that a forgiving God will not give up hope or abandon them.

How surprised Jacob must have been to find that even at a temporary stop along the road God was present. "Surely the Lord is in this place and I was not aware of it," Jacob declares. We should remember that God is often much nearer than we think. As the rabbis of old put it: "Where does God dwell? In every heart that lets Him in."

JACOB'S TWO WIVES

RACHEL *and* LEAH
GENESIS 29–30:24

" While he was still talking with them, Rachel came with
her father's sheep, for she was a shepherdess. "
GENESIS 29:9

AFTER HIS DREAM at Bethel, Jacob continued his journey to the home of his uncle Laban in Haran, in Mesopotamia. He arrived at a field in the region, where he found shepherds standing by a well that was covered with a large stone. Jacob discovered that the men were from Haran and knew his uncle. While they were speaking, a young shepherdess approached the well with a flock of sheep. The shepherds identified her as Rachel, Laban's daughter.

As Rachel drew near, Jacob heaved away the huge stone from the well and began to draw water for his uncle's sheep. Then he kissed Rachel and wept with emotion, explaining that he was her father's nephew. Rachel ran off in excitement to tell the news to her father, who responded in kind and hurried to greet his kinsman. Embracing and kissing Jacob, Laban took him home and declared that he was his own "flesh and blood."

Jacob stayed with Laban and at first worked for him for nothing. After a month, however, Laban insisted that he should pay Jacob some wages. Jacob replied that all he wanted was the hand of Rachel in marriage, and in return he would work for Laban for seven years. Laban agreed to the deal, telling Jacob that "it's better that I give her to you than to some other man."

Jacob worked for his uncle for the promised seven years, and his love for Rachel was such that the years seemed to him "like only a few days." When the time was up and he had completed his side of the bargain, Jacob asked Laban for his wife. Laban duly organized the wedding and the celebratory feast.

✠ *Marriage and children* ✠

On the night of the wedding, however, Laban betrayed his nephew. He sent in his older, less attractive daughter Leah to sleep with Jacob. Thinking that Leah was Rachel, Jacob slept with her, thus sealing his marriage to her. Only in the morning did he realize that he had been tricked. When Jacob confronted Laban with his treachery, his uncle replied: "It is not our custom here to give the younger daughter in marriage before the older one." He then told Jacob that after the week of festivities, he could also marry Rachel, if he agreed to work for him another seven years. Jacob consented; he took Rachel as his wife and loved her more than her sister.

God took pity on Leah's loveless marriage and blessed her with four sons: Reuben, Simeon, Levi, and Judah. Meanwhile, Rachel found that she was barren. Understandably, she became envious of her sister's fertility. So, just as Sarah had given Hagar to Abraham (pp. 16–19), Rachel gave her maidservant Bilhah to Jacob. Bilhah bore him two sons, Dan and Naphtali.

In time, Leah was unable to have more children, so she, too, gave her maidservant Zilpah to Jacob. This resulted in the birth of two sons, Gad and Asher. Later, Leah's prayers for fertility were

granted by God and she bore two more sons, Issachar and Zebulun, and a daughter named Dinah. Finally, "God remembered Rachel…and opened her womb," and she gave birth to Joseph, who would become greater than all his brothers.

✠ Jacob meets his match ✠

When Jacob met Laban, he encountered for the first time someone as crafty as himself. His uncle's trickery recalls, with some irony, Jacob's own deception of his brother Esau and his

Jacob kisses Rachel at their first meeting, in this 19th-century painting by Joseph Ritter van Führich. The shepherds are those who informed Jacob that he had reached the region where his uncle Laban lived.

father Isaac. The story also echoes Abraham's search for a wife for Isaac through his chief servant (pp. 32–35). Just as Abraham's servant first saw Rebekah at a well, so Jacob first met Rachel at one. In each instance, the bride-to-be ran off in excitement to tell Laban of her encounter. But whereas Abraham's servant came bearing gifts as a bride-price for Rebekah, Jacob had nothing to offer Laban but manual labor.

Seven years' work was a high price for a bride, and Laban was quick to exploit Jacob's ardent desire for Rachel; ironically, the situation bears a resemblance to the time when Jacob used Esau's physical hunger to his advantage (pp. 38–41). But instead of securing a birthright, Laban devised a plan to marry off Leah and secure Jacob's services for another seven years – a plan that would have done justice to Jacob and his scheming mother. In fact, Jacob's failure to identify Leah – whether because it was dark, Leah was veiled, or he had drunk too much – and his unwitting consummation of an unwanted marriage recall the way in which Jacob tricked his blind father into blessing him by pretending to be Esau. When Laban

Jacob raises the stone that covered a well of water so his uncle's sheep could drink, in this 14th-century stone relief from Salisbury Cathedral in England.

informed Jacob that it was customary for the older daughter to marry before the younger, his words must have been an uncomfortable reminder for Jacob of how he, the younger brother, had stolen the birthright and blessing of Esau. The tables had truly been turned.

> ❝ *But when evening came, he took his daughter Leah and gave her to Jacob, and Jacob lay with her.* ❞
>
> GENESIS 29:23

But if the story illustrates how Jacob – at least initially – met his match in Laban, it also shows some of the qualities that would eventually make him a worthy successor to Abraham. His love for Rachel – demonstrated by his willingness to labor

An Israeli girl tends livestock in the Judean Hills, west of Hebron. As Jacob had practiced (Genesis 30:32), sheep and goats are being raised together. Jacob cared for his uncle Laban's flocks during his stay in Haran.

for his uncle for 14 years without wages — revealed his true capacity for a deep and pure emotion unsullied by his natural wildness. His decision to work for seven years before marrying Rachel was also indicative of his determination and patience — qualities that Esau notably lacked. In addition, although Jacob was angry at Laban's treachery, he accepted his uncle's offer to work for another seven years without plotting a murderous revenge, as was Esau's intention.

Yet it is possible that Jacob vented his anger and frustration in a more subtle way — by denying Leah his affection. Genesis states simply that he "loved Rachel more than Leah" and that "the Lord saw that Leah was not loved."

Although Leah had suffered from her loveless marriage, she was rewarded by God with children. Genesis again shows His compassion for those who, like Hagar and Ishmael (pp. 24–25), are rejected. Indeed, Leah became the mother of six of the founding fathers of the 12 tribes of Israel. Among these was Judah, whose line included King David and, ultimately, Jesus Christ himself. ▲

MESSAGE
—for—
TODAY

LIFE WAS DIFFICULT *for Jacob during his extended stay with his uncle. Laban did provide him with lodging and work, but seven years of manual labor to earn a wife was not generous terms — and even then, Laban deceived Jacob when his reward came due. Laban also changed Jacob's wages 10 times (Genesis 31:41), apparently not to Jacob's advantage. Individuals who find themselves in desperate circumstances will recognize that Jacob had little choice but to keep working under unfavorable terms. Yet his love for Rachel so filled him with hope and optimism that seven years seemed like only a few days.*

God's provision for us in the midst of hardship may not be what we would choose for ourselves. But we can be sure that as we accept His provision with trust and hope, God will work for our good.

RETURNING *to* CANAAN

The FLIGHT *from* LABAN
GENESIS 30:25–31:55

> *Jacob said to Laban, 'Send me on my way so that*
> *I can go back to my own homeland.'*
> GENESIS 30:25

SOME TIME AFTER Rachel had given birth to Joseph, Jacob decided to return to Canaan. When his uncle Laban – whose livestock had prospered under his nephew – heard of his intentions, he asked Jacob what he could give him to make him stay. Jacob replied that he would work for a further period if Laban gave him the speckled goats and sheep and the black lambs from his stock. Laban agreed. He then promptly removed these animals from his livestock and pastured them out of Jacob's reach, a three-day journey away. Jacob, however, countered his uncle's treachery by producing his own flock of speckled animals through a method of stockbreeding.

As Jacob's flock grew in size, and with it his prosperity, Laban and his sons became increasingly resentful. At this point, God told Jacob directly: "Go back to the land of your fathers and to your relatives, and I will be with you." So Jacob summoned Rachel and Leah and told them how his relationship with their father Laban had deteriorated. He also recounted a dream in which God had revealed His part in creating livestock for Jacob at the expense of Laban's flocks. Finally, Jacob told his wives how God had commanded him to leave for Canaan.

The two women, already angry that their father had withheld their dowry money, told Jacob to do whatever God said. So Jacob loaded up his camels with his wives, children, and goods, and gathering together all his animals, he fled.

Unknown to Jacob, Rachel had stolen her father's "household gods"; these were small pagan idols that she had secretly placed among her belongings.

✾ A confrontation and covenant ✾

Laban discovered Jacob's departure three days later. He immediately gave chase and, after a week's pursuit, caught up with his nephew near Gilead, southeast of the Sea of Galilee. He set up his tents opposite Jacob's and prepared to confront the younger man. But before he could do so, God appeared to Laban in a dream and warned him not to "say anything to Jacob, either good or bad."

Laban visited Jacob and accused him of running away with his daughters without letting him say goodbye and of stealing his household gods. Jacob replied that they departed in secret because he feared Laban would keep his daughters from him. Unaware of Rachel's theft, Jacob denied taking Laban's gods and said that if he found them on anyone in his household, that person would die. Laban searched Jacob's tent, as well as those of Leah and two maidservants, but found nothing. He then entered Rachel's tent. But Rachel was sitting on a saddle in which she had hidden the gods. Claiming that she had her period, Rachel told her father that she could not stand up and watched while he searched her tent in vain.

Feeling vindicated by Laban's failure to find his gods, Jacob angrily took his uncle to task for accusing him of the theft. He reminded Laban of

Jacob's flight from Laban is depicted in this 16th-century fresco by Raphael. Jacob's wives and children traveled on camels, and the livestock preceded the group.

how he had toiled for him for over 14 years: "The heat consumed me in the daytime and the cold at night, and sleep fled from my eyes." Laban, Jacob said, had changed his wages 10 times and would have sent him away with nothing if he had not had the protection of God.

At last, Laban offered to make a covenant, or treaty, with his nephew. Jacob agreed to this; he set up a pillar and arranged for stones to be piled up in a heap beside it. Laban then swore with God as his witness that he would respect the pillar and the cairn of stones as a boundary line that he would not cross to harm Jacob; Jacob swore to do likewise and promised to take care of Laban's daughters and never to marry another woman. The next day, Laban kissed and blessed his daughters and grandchildren and returned to his home.

✡ Fleeing from toil ✡

With Jacob's flight from Laban, another phase of his life came to a close. Initially, Jacob had left Canaan to escape the consequences of his treachery toward his brother Esau. Now,

Ba'al was a popular Canaanite god of rainfall and fertility. This bronze-and-gold statue of him (1400–1200 BC) is representative of the household gods Rachel stole from her father.

having suffered from Laban's own deviousness and rapacity, Jacob was making his way back to Canaan. One important difference exists between the two situations. In the first case, Jacob's mother Rebekah had urged him to leave home; this time, it was God Himself who told Jacob to return to his parents' home in Canaan. On Jacob's previous journey to Haran, God had promised to provide protection until he returned to Canaan. There, Jacob could claim the land promised to him and his descendants in God's covenant (Genesis 28:15).

For 14 years, Jacob had patiently worked for Laban in all conditions, suffering his uncle's capricious decisions to "change" – the implication is "reduce" – his wages. Although God apparently had not spoken directly to Jacob since the revelatory dream at Bethel, He saw how Laban treated Jacob, and He strengthened Jacob's flock at the expense of Laban's. As Jacob prepared to leave, his stoicism was further rewarded by a revelation from God, who promised to be with him.

✡ *Stealing the gods* ✡

Before Jacob and his family departed for Canaan, Rachel stole her father's household gods. The Hebrew word for these gods, *teraphim,* appears 15 times in the Old Testament and seems to refer to the statues of gods that provided the focus of family worship among pagan peoples.

Although typically small – thus Rachel could hide them in her saddle – they could also be as large as a person (1 Samuel 19:13). Scholars continue to puzzle over the motives for her theft. According to inscribed tablets found at the ancient Hurrian town of Nuzi in Mesopotamia, the possession of these gods may have carried with it a right of inheritance, which would explain Rachel's desire to have them. Conversely, the *teraphim* may have been thought to confer safety, prosperity, or even fertility. In any case, Rachel evidently had not totally broken free from her pagan background.

> ❝ *When Laban had gone to shear his sheep, Rachel stole her father's household gods.* ❞
> GENESIS 31:19

After describing Laban's unsuccessful search for the gods, Genesis concludes the story with a treaty. Laban and Jacob ratified the pact by placing stones in a "heap," each giving it an Aramaic and a Hebrew name, and declaring it a "witness," or memorial, to their agreement. Genesis records that the pile of stones, or cairn, was also called *mizpah,* meaning "watchtower." This indicated that God would stand guard at the stones to guarantee that each side kept the treaty. It is not clear why Laban was so anxious to have the treaty; Jacob was obviously heading away from his uncle's territory in Mesopotamia toward Canaan. However, the pact may look forward to a later period in history, when the Israelites and the Arameans were rivals, and the visible boundary line between their territories became important.

After establishing the treaty, Jacob made a sacrifice to God and shared a meal with Laban – the traditional way of sealing a treaty at that time. If mutual affection had escaped them, at least the two men's relationship had been restored, and Laban could give a farewell blessing to his daughters and grandchildren. For his part, Jacob continued his journey home, as God had directed. ▲

The Euphrates River, the longest river in western Asia, winds its way through Syria to the Persian Gulf. Jacob and his family crossed this river to escape from Laban.

MESSAGE
—for—
TODAY

THE COMMON TENDENCY of many people to think that they are right and that others are wrong is highlighted in this episode. Laban is angry that Jacob has left his home; Jacob is furious that Laban should think he had stolen his idols. Laban conveniently forgets how inhospitable he was to Jacob, and Jacob ignores the fact that he had acted like a thief, sneaking away without a word. Rachel is also at fault, of course, for taking her father's idols and then refusing to admit to the deed.

Although a treaty of peace officially patched up the family rift, no one confessed to his or her fault, and the peace amounted only to the absence of strife. Without honesty, remorse, and forgiveness, there can be no true reconciliation. Although God would fulfill His promises to and through Jacob, Jacob and his family had yet to learn how to behave honorably.

The MAN at the FORD

JACOB WRESTLES *with* GOD
GENESIS 32

" So Jacob was left alone, and a man wrestled with him till daybreak. "
GENESIS 32:24

FTER MAKING A PACT with Laban at Gilead, Jacob continued toward Canaan. He was encouraged by a meeting with angels at a place called Mahanaim (the exact site is disputed, but it is near the Jabbok River). Before he entered Canaan, Jacob knew he had to face up to and restore his relationship with his brother Esau, who now lived in Edom, southeast of the Dead Sea. So when Jacob reached the Jabbok River, a tributary of the Jordan River, he sent messengers to Esau to tell him that he hoped to "find favor in your eyes."

The messengers returned with the report that Esau was advancing to meet Jacob with 400 men. Fearful of Esau's intentions, Jacob divided his people and livestock into two groups: if Esau attacked one group, he reasoned, the other might escape. He prayed for God's help, and at intervals he sent Esau gifts of various herds and flocks.

Jacob sent his family across the Jabbok at night, while he stayed alone on the northern side. Then, Genesis records, a "man" appeared, and they wrestled until daybreak. The man could not overcome Jacob in the struggle, so he "touched the socket of Jacob's hip," dislocating it. Even so, Jacob clung to him until daybreak. At this point, the man ordered Jacob to let him go, but Jacob refused to do so unless the man blessed him. The stranger asked Jacob his name. On receiving a reply, the stranger told Jacob he would now be called Israel, because "you have struggled with God and with men and have overcome." When

An angel wrestles with Jacob, in this 19th-century German woodcut by Gustave Doré. Because he could not defeat him, the angel blessed Jacob and called him Israel, meaning "he struggles with God" or "God strives."

Jacob asked the man his name, he refused to divulge it, but he did give Jacob a blessing. Jacob renamed the place Peniel, "face of God," because he had seen God face to face. The episode ends with Jacob limping away.

✡ Jacob struggles with God ✡

As Jacob prepared to face his past in the form of a potentially hostile force, he realized he needed God. So he prayed to the Lord. Jacob declared that he was unworthy, showing uncharacteristic humility. But if in his distress he sought divine aid, he was also prepared to use his own resourcefulness; he decided to gain favor with his brother by sending gifts to him.

The encounter with the "man" at the ford has several strands to it. It shows how the place — which was probably a sacred Canaanite site at the time — came to be named Peniel. It also links the dislocation of Jacob's hip joint with a later Israelite prohibition: the Israelites "do not eat the tendon attached to the socket of the hip."

In addition, the encounter marks another milestone in Jacob's relationship with God. Some scholars think the stranger was the guardian spirit of the ford or an angel. It was clear to Jacob that the man must have supernatural power, for he dislocated a joint with a mere touch. Jacob also knew that the blessing of this man — whom he thought was God — was worth struggling for, even if the stranger would not reveal his identity.

For the Hebrews, a person's name indicates his character. When the "man" blessed Jacob and renamed him Israel, it effectively meant that God was confirming Jacob's worthiness to receive the promises given to Abraham and Isaac.

As Israel, Jacob gave his name to the Jewish people. His struggle with God would epitomize their belief that their trials were sent by God, and that God would also deliver them from the trials. In this way, Jacob emerged from the encounter with a new identity, ready now to face his brother and to enter Canaan, the Promised Land. ▲

MESSAGE
— for —
TODAY

FOR JACOB, this was the moment of truth — he was about to face up to his selfish actions. He had been running away from his past for more than 14 years — from the home where he had disgraced himself and from the brother he had cheated. Now Jacob was about to confront Esau, who would either want to harm him or gladly welcome him home.

It was while Jacob pondered his fate that a mysterious man struggled with him. He might have been a messenger from God sent to test Jacob, but some have suggested that the story describes Jacob wrestling with himself, trying to decide whether he trusted the God of his fathers or not. The struggle left him with a limp, but also with a new confidence. It is when we face our own biggest failures that we may be readiest to accept God's forgiveness and His greatest blessings.

A HAPPY REUNION

The MEETING with ESAU
GENESIS 33

> '*For to see your face is like seeing the face of God, now that you have received me favorably.*'
> GENESIS 33:10

AFTER JACOB HAD wrestled God, he rejoined his family and waited for the arrival of his brother Esau with his 400 men. Not knowing what to expect from his brother, Jacob arranged his household in readiness for a possible attack when Esau came into view. He placed his wives' two maidservants with their children at the front, put Leah and her children behind them, and finally, positioned his favorites, Rachel and her son Joseph, in the rear.

As soon as Esau arrived, Jacob walked out alone and "bowed down to the ground seven times" before him. Any fears Jacob might have had were quickly dispelled when Esau ran up to his brother and kissed and hugged him. Both of them were emotional and wept for joy. At this point, Esau looked up and saw Jacob's family, and he asked who they were. Jacob replied that "they are the children God has graciously given your servant." The wives and children walked up to Esau and bowed down. Esau then wanted to know why Jacob had sent him the droves of animals. On hearing they were a gift, Esau refused to accept them – until Jacob insisted he should take them.

Esau then suggested that they should leave together for his home in Seir, or Edom, to the south. But Jacob knew his destiny lay in Canaan, not Seir. He told his brother that he would follow him slowly since "the children are tender and…I must care for the ewes and cows that are nursing their young." Esau agreed to this and offered him an escort of men, which Jacob declined.

Believing that Jacob was right behind him, Esau left for Seir. Meanwhile, Jacob and his family went in their own direction, to the west, and pitched their tents at Succoth. They then crossed the Jordan River and traveled to Shechem, where Jacob purchased a plot of ground for 100 pieces of

Jacob bowing before his brother Esau in humility is illustrated in this 19th-century German painting by Julius Schnorr von Carolsfeld.

silver. There, "he set up an altar and called it El Elohe Israel," which is Hebrew for "God, the God of Israel."

✡ Returning the blessing ✡

Although Esau's 400 men might have been an escort designed to impress his brother, Jacob took no chances. He tried to shield his family – especially his favorites, Rachel and Joseph – from a possible attack. He then stepped out in front to meet Esau, bowing to show his humility. But Jacob's fears were swept away by his brother's effusive welcome. In a scene that some scholars believe Jesus had in mind when he described the reunion between the Prodigal Son and his father (Luke 15:20), the two brothers clasped each other, shedding tears of joy. In moments, they purged the guilt and resentment that had been festering for more than 14 years.

To seal their reconciliation, Jacob insisted that Esau keep the animals he had given as a present to him. Seeing Esau's face, Jacob declared, was "like seeing the face of God," a reference to his meeting with God at Peniel ("face of God"). The Hebrew word for "present" can also mean "blessing." This can be seen, for example, when Isaac told Esau: "Your brother came deceitfully and took your blessing [Genesis 27:35]." In a way, Jacob was returning to Esau the blessing, embodied by the present of livestock.

Despite the brothers' reconciliation, Jacob knew his destiny was not with Esau in Seir. Jacob pretended he would follow his brother but intended to go to Succoth in the Jordan Valley. Though his means were dubious, his end – his return to Canaan – accorded with God's purpose. At Shechem, back on Canaanite soil, Jacob bought land and raised an altar to God. By calling it El Elohe Israel, he showed that he recognized that God had kept His promise made at Bethel, to bring Jacob back safely to Canaan (Genesis 28:15). He acknowledged that the Lord – the God of his forefathers – was Israel's God as well. ▲

MESSAGE
—for—
TODAY

Ordinary people can be capable of extraordinary behavior. Jacob may have been one of the Patriarchs and Esau his foolish brother, but it is Esau who takes the lead and shows the way of forgiveness. Despite being cheated of his birthright, Esau harbors no bitterness toward his brother. His willingness to forgive provides an example in reconciliation for other families whose lives have been disrupted by disputes. And his uncomplicated response to his brother's return shows a humility often praised in the Scriptures.

Jacob declined Esau's offer to travel together with a lie. Old habits of deception had apparently taken such a hold of Jacob that he could not accept his brother's love. When we find old bad habits following us through life, it is time to humbly acknowledge them. Then God can help us change.

VIOLENT REVENGE

DINAH and the SHECHEMITES
GENESIS 34

66 *They were filled with grief and fury, because Shechem had done a disgraceful thing in Israel by lying with Jacob's daughter — a thing that should not be done.* 99
GENESIS 34:7

JACOB AND HIS HOUSEHOLD were staying near the city of Shechem, in Canaan, when his daughter Dinah decided to visit some of the local women who had become her friends. The gesture ended in a tremendous disaster for the Shechemites. On her way to the town, Dinah came across Shechem, the son of Hamor – the "ruler of that area." Burning with lust for the young woman, Shechem seized and raped her. After he had satisfied his desire, however, he realized that his attraction for the girl went beyond the physical; in fact, he was in love with Dinah. So Shechem asked his father to obtain Jacob's permission for him to marry Dinah.

Meanwhile, news of the rape had reached Jacob. He reacted with considerable calm. Instead of running out to tell his sons, who were working in the fields, he waited until they came home. His sons, however, quickly learned what had happened and immediately rushed home. When they arrived, "filled with grief and fury," they saw Hamor and Shechem talking with their father.

Hamor tried to calm their rage, assuring them that his son loved Dinah and wanted to marry her. He proposed further that Jacob's family should intermarry with the people of the city: "You can settle among us; the land is open to you. Live in it, trade in it, and acquire property in it."

Shechem then asked in a conciliatory tone that he might "find favor" in their eyes; he was willing to pay whatever they asked, he said, as a bride-price for Dinah.

✡ A deceitful reply ✡

Dinah's brothers were not mollified by the words offered by Shechem. In fact, they plotted revenge for his disgraceful actions. For the moment, however, the brothers pretended to agree with Hamor and Shechem's proposal. They said they would consent to intermarriage but only on one condition. The brothers wanted every one of the male citizens of Shechem to be circumcised: "Then we will give you our daughters and take your daughters for ourselves."

Hamor and Shechem believed Jacob's sons, so they agreed to the condition; and Shechem, eager to be united with Dinah, wasted no time in undergoing the ritual. But the two men still had to persuade their fellow citizens. They went to the gate of the city – where legal matters were usually dealt with – and spoke to the other male citizens there, explaining that Jacob and his sons were friendly. There was plenty of land to accommodate all of Jacob's family, and if they did so, Jacob's property, livestock, and other animals would become theirs.

Swayed by their words, all the men of the city agreed to the proposal and underwent circumcision. Three days later, while the Shechemites were still in great discomfort from the operation,

Dinah tries to rebuke Shechem's advances, in this illustration from a 15th-century German manuscript. By defiling the daughter of Leah and Jacob, the young man caused strife between Jacob's family and the Shechemites.

Simeon and Levi, two of Dinah's brothers, attacked and killed every male, including Hamor and Shechem. Afterward, the other brothers looted the city, seizing the livestock, donkeys, and the women and children.

When his sons returned to their tents with their booty, Jacob berated Simeon and Levi for their violent, irresponsible act, which, he said, would make them notorious among the people of Canaan. He pointed out that they were few in number compared with the other Canaanite tribes. If the Canaanites were to unite against Jacob, he and all his household could be wiped out. The two brothers, however, were unrepentant, telling their father: "Should he have treated our sister like a prostitute?"

✡ A conflict of morality ✡

Ironically, if Jacob had not broken his word to Esau and had followed his brother to Seir as agreed, the tragedy and slaughter of this episode would never have taken place. The rape of Dinah and the violent revenge taken by her brothers is one of the grimmest episodes in Genesis. Except for the tender words spoken by Shechem to Dinah after he had violated her, the motifs are violence, greed, and deviousness.

Some scholars believe the story may reflect a historical occasion when the tribes of Simeon and Levi – personalized as the two brothers themselves – tried to settle at Shechem. Others point out that the vividness of the account suggests that it was based on an actual incident.

This gold and silver "knife" from a tomb in Byblos is one of two types of swords – short and long – used in the 18th century BC. This short sword may be similar to one used at Shechem.

All that remains of Shechem are these temple ruins, dating from 1500–1300 BC, near the modern city of Nablus. In Jacob's time, Shechem was an important city because of its location on a main route through Palestine.

The episode is more than a straightforward tale of rape and revenge, however. It sets out the moral complexities of the incident in such a way that it is difficult to condemn or condone completely the characters involved. Shechem, as the son of the ruler, may have been immune from the consequences of his actions in his time and culture, although today he would be the clear-cut villain. But after the rape, Genesis spells out his affection for Dinah: "He loved the girl and spoke tenderly to her." Nevertheless, to Jacob's sons, all his subsequent affection could not atone for his crime.

In later times, the Jewish Law specified punishments for rapists: "If a man happens to meet a virgin who is not pledged to be married and rapes her and they are discovered, he shall pay the girl's father 50 shekels of silver. He must marry the girl, for he has violated her. He can never divorce her as long as he lives [Deutcronomy 22:28–29]."

> 'You have brought trouble on me by making me a stench to the Canaanites...'
>
> GENESIS 34:30

In this situation, although Shechem wanted to marry Dinah and was prepared to pay a generous bride-price, her brothers proposed that the entire male population be circumcised – an action that would temporarily incapacitate them. The greedy Shechemites sealed their own fate through their desire to lay their hands on Jacob's vast property and livestock. In pain after their circumcision, they were easy prey for Simeon and Levi, who, as sons of Leah, were full brothers of Dinah and probably felt her violation the most keenly.

Jacob was angry not so much for the bloodshed itself, but for the damage it had done to their tribe's reputation in Canaan and the possibility that it might provoke a reprisal. Jacob later punished the two brothers when, on his deathbed, he pronounced that their descendants would be scattered far and wide over Canaan (Genesis 49:7).

Genesis suggests that the Jacob who had been strengthened and given a new identity at Peniel and who had just bravely confronted his brother Esau was now backsliding into moral apathy. Conversely, if Jacob's response was based more on pragmatism than on outrage at the rape of his daughter, Simeon and Levi are shown to have taken righteous anger and the defense of family honor to an indefensible extreme. Yet despite the split in the family and the moral failings on both sides, God would still keep His promise to protect them and lead them south to Bethel. ▲

MESSAGE
—for—
TODAY

NO ONE BUT THE ORIGINAL victim Dinah comes out well in this episode. Shechem violated Dinah. The fact that he subsequently loved her and was willing to adopt her faith does not excuse his crime. However disgraceful Shechem's treatment of their sister, Simeon and Levi were wrong to respond with slaughter. Jacob, too, takes a questionable stance. Instead of being concerned with the immorality of his sons' murderous actions, he worries about the trouble it could cause him.

The text clearly shows the price of acting irresponsibly. Not once did anyone ask God for wisdom. While the Bible offers us actions to emulate, it also shows us faults to avoid. Being human means having both strengths and faults; being faithful means asking God for help to distinguish between the two so that we can choose the right course.

COMING HOME

JACOB RETURNS *to* BETHEL
GENESIS 35

> ❝ *'Go up to Bethel and settle there, and build an altar there to God, who appeared to you...'* ❞
>
> GENESIS 35:1

AFTER THE EVENTS at Shechem, God told Jacob to go south to Bethel, where he had received his first divine revelations, and to build an altar for Him. Jacob made preparations immediately for the move. He ordered his household to get rid of their "foreign gods," purify themselves ritually, and put on new clothes. When his family and servants handed over their statues of pagan gods and "the rings in their ears" worn as charms, Jacob buried them under an oak tree by the city.

With the rituals over, Jacob left for Bethel. He might have expected an attack from neighbors of the Shechemites after the slaughter, but the "terror of God fell upon the towns." So Jacob reached Bethel safely and built an altar to God. He named the place El Bethel, "God of Bethel," because it was there that God had appeared to him when he was fleeing from Esau (pp. 42–43).

God again spoke to Jacob, reaffirming that his name would from now on be Israel. God reiterated

Megalithic stone pillars (c. 20th–17th century BC) still stand in what was ancient Canaan. They were used as altars, and such offerings as wine were poured on them. Jacob erected pillars to mark where God spoke to him.

His covenant promises made to Abraham: Jacob would give rise to a "nation and a community of nations"; kings would "come from [his] body"; and the land God had promised to his forefathers would be granted to Jacob's descendants. After God had spoken, Jacob set up a stone pillar and anointed it with a "drink offering" and oil.

Jacob's family then traveled to Mamre near Hebron, where his father Isaac lived. En route, Rachel died as she gave birth to Benjamin and was buried near Ephrath (Bethlehem). After Jacob arrived at Mamre, Isaac passed away at the age of 180, and he was buried by Esau and Jacob in the family tomb (pp. 30–31).

✡ Worshiping God Almighty ✡

Before departing for Bethel, Jacob insisted that his family and servants purify themselves, perhaps because they were defiled by the spilling of blood at Shechem. He also ordered a purge of pagan idols – evidence that his household still had objects of popular folk religion and superstition. Indeed, Rachel's theft of her father's household gods (pp. 48–51) may well reflect the attraction these pagan idols continued to exert.

It was also at Shechem that Joshua, who would lead the Israelites into the Promised Land in later times, warned of the dangers of idoltary: "If you forsake the Lord and serve foreign gods, He will turn and bring disaster on you…[Joshua 24:20]." By getting rid of the idols, Jacob made it clear that the God who had brought him safely to and back from his uncle's home in Haran was the only God to be worshiped.

So, with the Lord's protection, Jacob reached Bethel, marking the peak of his spiritual journey. God restated the promises of the covenant, adding that Jacob would be the ancestor of kings. Royal descendants had been promised to Abraham (Genesis 17:6) but not to Jacob, until now. God also confirmed his name as Israel. The revelation sustained him throughout his life, and he referred to it on his deathbed (Genesis 48:3–4). ▲

MESSAGE
— for —
TODAY

WHEN A PERSON changes his or her name, it often signifies a change of identity – whether adopting a new faith or entering a marriage. Jacob's change of name is equally significant. The Hebrew word "Jacob" literally means "heel" and referred to Jacob's birth, when he came out of his mother's womb clutching Esau's heel. It also carries the sense of "being a heel" – a cheat – a trait that had characterized much of Jacob's life in the past.

Now, however, Jacob was confirmed as "Israel," which literally means "he struggles with God." Jacob has struggled with himself and faced up to his responsibilities. The trickster has finally become the Patriarch. Like Israel, none of us needs to be condemned to a lifetime of old faults repeating themselves. In faith, we can shake off our past and humbly seek a better future with God's help.

THE STORY OF JOSEPH

A MODEL of VIRTUE
GENESIS 37–50

> **"** *'Can we find anyone like this man, one in whom is the spirit of God?'* **"**
>
> GENESIS 41:38

Genesis tells of the life of Joseph, Jacob's second youngest son and the first-born of Jacob's favored wife, Rachel. These episodes bring the age of the Patriarchs to a closing and explain how the children of Israel became inhabitants of Egypt. They also provide the background for the Book of Exodus, which describes how Moses led the children of Israel out of slavery in Egypt.

Joseph's story lacks some of the features of the Abraham and Jacob cycles – notably the direct appearances of God and incidents that explain the origins of place names. In fact, because of its strong unity of style and considerable literary skill, many modern scholars have described it as a novella.

According to Genesis, Joseph was his father's favorite son – a prime factor behind the hatred that fueled his brothers' decision to sell him as a slave to merchants heading for Egypt. In Egypt, Pharaoh and his subjects were greatly aided by Joseph's ability to

Joseph, the son of the Patriarch Jacob, is depicted in this detail from a 17th-century Italian painting by Guido Reni. Joseph lived most of his life in Egypt and died at the age of 110.

interpret dreams. Realizing that God was guiding Joseph, Pharaoh made him prime minister, or vizier. Joseph predicted the great famine that struck the whole of the Middle East and forced Joseph's brothers to come from Canaan to Egypt in search of food. Joseph recognized them but concealed his true identity until he saw that they were remorseful for their evil deed. Eventually, Joseph obtained Pharaoh's permission to settle Jacob and the rest of his family in the fertile region of the Nile River.

✡ A virtuous Patriarch ✡

Although scholars have tried to fit Joseph's life into a period of Egyptian history, the lack of evidence has weighed against them. The Genesis account does not name the Egyptian pharaoh, for example, and historians have yet to come across an Egyptian vizier with a name resembling Joseph's in Egyptian records. Some scholars, however, believe that Joseph may have lived at a time when a dynasty of Semitic rulers, known to the Egyptians as the Hyksos, were governing the country (c. 1663–1555 BC) from their capital of Avaris (also known as Rameses) in the Nile delta.

Joseph is one of the most virtuous characters of the Old Testament. He was a victim of blatant injustice – both when his brothers sold him into slavery and when, in Egypt, Potiphar's wife accused him falsely of rape. Yet he did not indulge in self-righteousness or self-pity; neither did he plan revenge, but instead he generously forgave his brothers. ▲

He also made the best of every situation – for example, during his long imprisonment in an Egyptian jail, when he put his ability to interpret dreams to good use.

Throughout his trials, Joseph was sustained by God's protection; and when the tide turned his way, he never doubted that the Lord lay behind his success. Indeed, his story is a witness to God's capacity for transforming evil – a theme that is summed up in Joseph's words to his brothers: "You intended to harm me, but God intended it for good." ▲

Joseph, as a member of a nomadic farming family, initially lived in Canaan. His brothers sold him to merchants, who took him to Egypt along one of the traditional trading routes – the exact one is not known. Joseph's family later joined him there and settled in Goshen. Joseph remained in Egypt until his death.

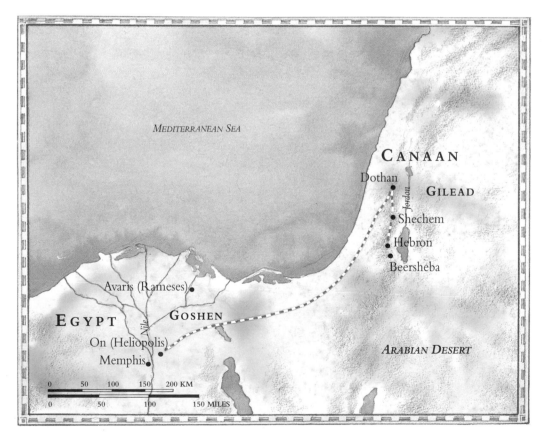

SOLD into SLAVERY

JOSEPH and his BROTHERS
GENESIS 37

> ❝ *'Listen to this dream I had: We were binding sheaves of grain out in the field when suddenly my sheaf rose and stood upright, while your sheaves gathered round mine and bowed down to it.'* ❞
> GENESIS 37:7

WHEN GENESIS INTRODUCES the most important part of his story, Joseph, Jacob's second youngest son, is 17 years of age. At the time, he was living with his family in the land of Canaan, to which Jacob had returned after the slaughter of the Shechemites. Jacob much preferred Joseph – the first of his two sons by his late beloved wife Rachel – to his other 11 sons. As a token of his special affection, Jacob gave Joseph a "richly ornamented robe" – traditionally translated as a "coat of many colors."

But Jacob's favoritism caused jealousy among his other sons, who were openly hostile to Joseph. They became even more resentful when on one occasion, Joseph related to them a dream that he had had: while they were all binding sheaves of grain in a field, Joseph's sheaf stood upright and his brothers' sheaves bowed down to it. The brothers interpreted the dream as saying that Joseph would rise to rule over them, and so they "hated him all the more." To make matters worse, Joseph had another dream, in which the sun, moon, and 11 stars bowed down to him. This time, even his father Jacob was upset, believing that this dream was suggesting that he and his wife Leah would also have to pay homage to Joseph.

Some time after the two dreams, Joseph was sent by Jacob to check on the well-being of his brothers, who were grazing their flocks in the fields near Shechem. When Joseph arrived at the fields, a man told him that his brothers had moved the flocks to Dothan, about 15 miles (25 km) to the north, and so Joseph set out to find them.

When the brothers saw him approaching from the distance, they decided they would get rid of Joseph once and for all. They planned to kill him and throw his body into an empty water cistern. The eldest brother Reuben, however, tried to dissuade the others from murdering Joseph in cold blood. They should simply throw him into the cistern, he said. (Meanwhile, Reuben secretly planned to rescue Joseph later.) The brothers agreed to this, and when Joseph arrived, they ripped off his ornamented robe, pushed him into the cistern, and with their treacherous deed accomplished, sat down to eat a meal.

✿ *The selling of Joseph* ✿

As the brothers were about to eat, a caravan of camels accompanied by Ishmaelite traders from Gilead came into view. The traders were heading for Egypt to sell their spices. When Judah, Leah's fourth son, saw them, he suggested that instead of letting Joseph die in the cistern, they should sell him as a slave to the merchants. His brothers agreed to this plan, and they pulled

Joseph up and sold him to the Ishmaelites for 20 shekels of silver.

After Joseph had been taken away, Reuben – who was probably tending the flocks while his brothers were eating – returned to find the empty cistern and was horrified. He confronted his brothers, who apparently realized at last that they would have to explain Joseph's absence to Jacob. So the brothers dipped his robe into the blood of

The merchants agree to purchase Joseph from his brothers, as depicted in this 19th-century painting by Friedrich Overbeck. To the Ishmaelites, Joseph was a commodity – he could be sold as a slave in Egypt.

a slaughtered goat and brought it back to Jacob, saying that Joseph had been killed by a wild animal. As they had hoped, Jacob was fooled by the bloody garment into thinking his favorite son was dead. Jacob was overcome with grief. Refusing to be comforted, he said he would mourn Joseph until the day he died. In the meantime, in Egypt, the Ishmaelites sold Joseph as a slave to Potiphar, the "captain of the guard," who was in the service of Pharaoh, the Egyptian ruler.

✡ *The favorite son* ✡

During his own upbringing, Jacob had suffered the effects of paternal favoritism, so he might have been expected to avoid repeating the pattern in his own family. However, his particular attachment to Joseph sowed the seeds of resentment in his other sons and set in motion the events that would take Joseph to Egypt.

For their part, Joseph's brothers disliked their younger sibling not only because of his preferred status but also because he "brought their father a bad report about them." But their hatred turned to treachery after Joseph described his two dreams. Later on, Joseph gained a respectable reputation in Egypt as an interpreter of dreams (pp. 70–73). At home, he did not have to explain

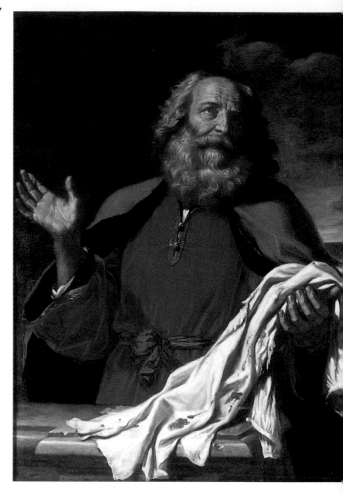

The blood-stained ornamented robe leaves Jacob in grief, as illustrated in this 16th-century Italian painting by Francesco Barbieri Guercino. The robe was dipped in goat's blood to convince Jacob that Joseph was dead.

Wheat is being harvested, in this 14th-century BC Egyptian wall painting. In Joseph's time, a sickle was used to cut the grain — wheat and barley were common — before the stalks were bound into bundles, or sheaves.

them. Their symbolism was ominously clear to his brothers and father.

Perhaps the brothers feared that Joseph's dreams would prove to be prophetic. When they were at Dothan, they abruptly decided to murder Joseph. Only Reuben — who as the eldest of the brothers would have borne the most responsibility for Joseph's death — and Judah prevailed upon the others not to kill Joseph. Their ultimate decision to sell Joseph to the Ishmaelites must have seemed an ideal solution to the brothers: they could rid themselves of Joseph, avoid the guilt of killing him, and be paid for the deed.

The Ishmaelites – who are also called Midianites and Medanites – were by tradition descendants of Abraham's son Ishmael. They had come from Gilead, a fertile region southeast of the Sea of Galilee, and their camels were laden with spices, balm, and myrrh (p. 80), which they were taking to Egypt along one of the traditional trading routes. Some of these ingredients were used by the Egyptians to preserve dead bodies for the afterlife. The person's corpse was dehydrated with natron salts and embalmed with resins and spices before being carefully wrapped in linen bandages. In fact, Joseph himself was embalmed, in the Egyptian manner, after his death (Genesis 50:26).

> **'Some ferocious animal has devoured him. Joseph has surely been torn to pieces.'**
> GENESIS 37:33

After they had sold Joseph into slavery, the brothers tricked their father into believing that he had been killed by a savage animal. Their deception recalls – with some irony – the episode when a youthful Jacob had used a stew of goat's meat to deceive his own father Isaac into blessing him instead of his older brother Esau (pp. 38–41). While Jacob "tore his clothes" and put on "sackcloth" to demonstrate his grief – these were traditional ritual expressions – Joseph began a new life in Egypt as a slave.

Although Joseph had been reduced to the lowest social position imaginable, his own two dreams provide a clue that behind the outward appearance of events, God was working out not only his destiny, but also that of his clan. At the right moment, the Lord's providential care would raise Joseph to a position of power that would cause his brothers to bow down to him – as the dream images of the sheaves and the sun, moon, and stars had foretold. ▲

MESSAGE
— for —
TODAY

JACOB SHOULD HAVE KNOWN from the experiences of his own childhood (pp. 38–41) the trouble that can be caused when parents have favorites. It was the brothers, not Joseph, who interpreted the dreams as signifying his future elevation – no doubt based on his preferred status in the family.

It's not hard to imagine how dramatic a change Joseph's life underwent, from favored son of a wealthy family to slavery in an alien land, utterly cut off, without hope of rescue. Yet Joseph responded by becoming a faithful servant, and his choice eventually served him well, because God had his rescue well in hand.

Although events in our lives may seem to be turning out for the worst, we should not give up our faith in God – He may be bringing us to a better future through our bad experiences.

A FALSE ACCUSATION

POTIPHAR'S WIFE

GENESIS 39

*" And though she spoke to Joseph day after day, he refused
to go to bed with her or even to be with her. "*

GENESIS 39:10

SOLD TO MERCHANTS, Joseph was taken to Egypt, where he was sold again as a slave to Potiphar, the captain of Pharaoh's guard. Through the blessing of God, everything that Joseph did in Egypt turned out well – so much so that Potiphar, although a pagan, discerned that the "Lord was with him." Eventually, Potiphar promoted Joseph to be his personal attendant and put him in charge of his entire estate. His decision was prudent, because "the blessing of the Lord was on everything Potiphar had, both in the house and in the field." Indeed, the Egyptian was so confident of Joseph's abilities that he handed over to him all his day-to-day responsibilities.

However, this period of harmony came to an unjust end when Potiphar's wife tried to seduce Joseph. Rejecting her direct request that he sleep with her, Joseph told the woman that her husband had trusted him with all his affairs: to sleep with her would be to both betray Potiphar and "sin against God." Nevertheless, Potiphar's wife was not deterred by Joseph's refusal and continued to try to seduce him, without success.

Finally, when no other servants were present, Potiphar's wife tried seducing him once more. Catching Joseph by his cloak, she implored him to go to bed with her – but he ran out, leaving his cloak in her hand. Scorned yet again, the woman decided to take her revenge. Brandishing Joseph's cloak, she summoned her servants and accused Joseph of trying to rape her, saying that he ran off only when she screamed. Later, she repeated the same story to her husband, who immediately threw Joseph into prison.

Even though Joseph had suffered a sudden change in his fortunes, the Lord was still with him

The predatory wife of Potiphar attempts to ensnare Joseph, in this 17th-century painting by Guido Reni. Although Joseph refused her, Potiphar's wife pulled away his cloak and used it falsely to prove an attack against her.

and "granted him favor in the eyes of the prison warden." In the way that Potiphar had initially rewarded Joseph for his competence and good sense, the warden also promoted him to a position in charge of all the other prisoners and made him "responsible for all that was done there."

✡ *The false accusation* ✡

The story of Joseph and Potiphar's wife shows how quickly Joseph's life could change. In fact, the plot of the episode resembles that of a popular Egyptian story known as "The Tale of Two Brothers," which dates back to at least the late 13th century BC. In the tale, a young man is approached by his elder brother's wife, who tries to seduce him. When rebuffed, the wife tells her husband that his brother tried to rape her. Eventually, the accused man persuades his brother of his innocence, and they are reconciled. Some scholars believe that the author of Genesis may have drawn on this tale for the Joseph story. Others believe the details are insufficiently similar and point out that the motif of the "spurned woman's revenge" is found in the literatures of other peoples.

The Genesis story shows that despite the downturn in Joseph's fortunes, God was near him, imbuing him with a calmness and authority that led to trust by both Potiphar and the warden. So it is no wonder that Potiphar "burned with anger" when presented with what seemed like strong evidence of his loyal servant's philandering.

Potiphar could have put Joseph to death. But, perhaps mindful of Joseph's hitherto impeccable behavior, he chose imprisonment – not the common prison but the king's prison, where inmates received better treatment. Without bemoaning his fate, Joseph made the most of his situation. His confinement led to his meeting Pharaoh's cupbearer, who would later be instrumental in gaining an audience for Joseph before Pharaoh. In this way, through divine providence, the jail became a stepping-stone to Joseph's elevation to power. ▲

MESSAGE
—*for*—
TODAY

WE NEVER FIND out the name of Potiphar's wife, even though she plays a decisive role in Joseph's career. Perhaps this was deliberate. Her name is irrelevant compared with what she represents – those individuals who put their personal gratification before vows and loyalty and the well-being of others. She also typifies the vindictiveness of those whose advances are rejected. The superficiality of their so-called love is indicated by the way in which it so quickly turns to loathing.

Potiphar's wife falsely accused Joseph of seduction, the very crime of which she herself was guilty. Yet throughout it all, Joseph refused to be drawn into evildoing. And in the end, Joseph was better placed for his eventual blessing, while Potiphar's wife was left with nothing more than an empty coat.

REVELATIONS of the FUTURE

JOSEPH INTERPRETS DREAMS

GENESIS 40–41

" Then Joseph said to them, 'Do not interpretations belong to God? Tell me your dreams.' "

GENESIS 40:8

AMONG THE OTHER prisoners Joseph encountered in the king's prison were Pharaoh's chief cupbearer and chief baker, who had somehow incurred the wrath of their master – Genesis does not say how. One night, after they had been in jail for some time, each had a powerful dream. In the morning, both men were eager to discover the meaning of their dreams, but there was no one available who could interpret them, and they became despondent. When Joseph discovered the reason for the two men's gloom, he told them that only God could interpret their dreams accurately. He offered to try to discover their meaning with the Lord's guidance.

The cupbearer was first to tell Joseph of his dream. He dreamed about a vine with three branches, bearing budding clusters of grapes. He picked and squeezed these grapes into a cup and gave it to Pharaoh. Without hesitating, Joseph told the cupbearer that the dream meant that within three days Pharaoh would restore him to his former position. In return for his interpretation, Joseph asked the man to remember him and show him kindness after he was freed.

After hearing such a favorable interpretation, the baker then described his dream to Joseph. He had three baskets of bread on his head, and in the top one birds were eating "all kinds of baked goods for Pharaoh." On this occasion, the interpretation was ominous. Within three days, Joseph said, Pharaoh would hang him on a tree, and birds would peck at his body.

As it turned out, three days later, Pharaoh celebrated his birthday and fulfilled Joseph's interpretations of the dreams by reappointing the cupbearer and hanging the baker. Although Joseph had asked the cupbearer to remember him after his release, it was not until two years later that the man eventually fulfilled his promise.

✿ Dreams of famine ✿

The cupbearer finally remembered Joseph when Pharaoh himself had two dreams that his Egyptian sages could not elucidate. In the first dream, Pharaoh was standing alongside the Nile River when seven fat, sleek cows emerged from the water. These were soon followed by seven gaunt cows, who ate the fat ones. In the second dream, Pharaoh saw seven full, healthy heads of grain growing from one stalk; however, "seven other heads of grain sprouted – thin and scorched by the east wind," and the thin heads "swallowed up" the full heads.

After hearing the dreams, the cupbearer told the Pharaoh about Joseph's gift for interpreting dreams. So the king sent for Joseph and asked him

what the dreams signified. Joseph replied that not he, but God, would give the answer. Both the dreams, he said, gave the same warning. The seven fat cows and seven full heads of grain represented seven years of abundant harvests throughout Egypt. The seven thin cows and seven thin heads of grain stood for seven years of famine.

Joseph added that Pharaoh should appoint a "discerning and wise man" to take charge of the country. Commissioners should be empowered to gather up and store a fifth of the harvest during the abundant years and hold it for the seven years of famine. Greatly impressed by Joseph's interpretations and authority, Pharaoh immediately made

The seated Pharaoh listens to Joseph's interpretation of his dreams, in this 19th-century French painting by Jean Adrien Guignet. Joseph's wisdom saved Egypt from famine and led to his appointment as governor.

him his second-in-command and gave him his own signet ring and a gold chain, along with white linen, to wear. He also gave Joseph an Egyptian name – Zaphenath-Paneah – and an Egyptian wife, Asenath, who was the daughter of a priest of the sun god Ra.

With his new responsibilities, Joseph, now 30 years of age, traveled around the country, organizing the collection of the grain and its storage in various cities. He gathered so much that "he stopped keeping records because it was beyond measure." Just as Joseph had predicted, the seven years of abundance came and went, followed by a severe famine that struck Egypt and the neighboring countries. But Joseph was so well organized that he could sell grain not only to Egyptians but also to foreigners.

✿ Interpreting through God ✿

Joseph's rise from prisoner to the second most powerful person in Egypt hinged on his ability to interpret dreams. Dream interpretation was widespread in the ancient Near East, especially in Egypt, where there was an extensive body of writings on the subject. Joseph, however, was distinguished from other interpreters because of his conviction that the answer to dream images could be found only through the inspiration of God, not in magical books. He made this clear to the cupbearer, to the baker, and to Pharaoh. Joseph trusted in the Lord to explain dreams.

Joseph languished in the prison for two years – a time that must have tested his faith and made him

wonder whether the cupbearer would remember him at all. His patient waiting was a test of character that his father and grandfather had also had to endure: Abraham for the birth of his and Sarah's son Isaac (pp. 16–19); and Jacob for his marriage to Rachel (pp. 44–47).

After he was freed, Joseph rose to a position of great power, one that is usually identified as that of vizier, or prime minister, of Egypt. The symbols of office that Pharaoh conferred on him are attested to elsewhere in Egyptian history. The signet ring carried the king's authority, fine white linen was the material of clothes worn at court, and a gold chain was the traditional sign of the king's approval. But despite his new status in Egyptian society, Joseph did not forget his roots. When his wife gave birth to two sons, he gave them the Hebrew names Manasseh and Ephraim.

As Joseph had predicted, the years of abundance arrived and were followed by famine.

An Egyptian pharaoh hunts ostrich in a horse-drawn chariot, in this 14th-century BC gold relief ornamentation. Joseph's chariot was given to him as a mark of power and prestige. Chariots were used in warfare and for sports.

The signet ring signifies Joseph's rise to Pharaoh's second-in-command. The ring given to him would have been similar to this Egyptian one, dating from the 13th century BC. The rings were engraved with an official seal, to be used as a signature.

Because of the annual flooding of the Nile River and its fertilization of the adjacent fields, Egypt was generally safeguarded against crop failure. Nevertheless, famine did occasionally occur there. One inscription, for example, records that a seven-year famine happened during the reign of Pharaoh Djoser (*c.* 2668–2649 BC) because of the Nile's failure to flood.

> **❝ *Pharaoh told them his dreams, but no one could interpret them for him.* ❞**
> GENESIS 41:8

When the famine did come, afflicting not only Egypt but "all the world" – that is, the ancient Middle East – Joseph was prepared for the crisis. Through his subsequent action he was able to partially fulfill God's promise to Abraham that "all peoples on Earth will be blessed through you [Genesis 12:3]." What Joseph might not have been ready for, however – since God had made him forget his "father's household" – was the impending arrival of his brothers. ▲

MESSAGE
—for—
TODAY

DREAMS HAD BEEN a source of trouble for Joseph and his brothers, but now they served to raise Joseph to leadership. Pharaoh believed Joseph's explanation of his dreams without waiting to see if they came to pass. Many interpretations had been offered, but only those of Joseph, who was following God's guidance, rang true.

Joseph suggested ways of meeting the approaching crisis. His advice included a job description that he himself fitted perfectly. Joseph was not just a man of God, but also a skillful entrepreneur who blended integrity with opportunism. As the first-century teacher Rabbi Hillel said, "If I am not for myself, who is for me? But if I am only for myself, what am I?" God can guide and bless us, and sometimes He does so through our own efforts. It is up to us to make the most of our opportunities when they arise.

The FIRST REUNION

JOSEPH'S BROTHERS VISIT EGYPT
GENESIS 42

" So Israel's sons were among those who went to buy grain,
for the famine was in the land of Canaan also. "
GENESIS 42:5

THE SEVERE FAMINE that Joseph had predicted from Pharaoh's dreams not only struck Egypt but also afflicted Canaan, including Jacob's household. When news filtered through to Jacob that Egypt had surplus stores of grain, he acted decisively, ordering his sons to go there and buy food "so that we may live and not die."

Joseph's 10 half-brothers set out for Egypt. Benjamin – Jacob's youngest son by his wife Rachel and Joseph's only full brother – stayed at home. His father did not want to risk his coming to any harm. When the brothers arrived in Egypt, they made their way to one of the cities that had stored grain – Genesis does not specify which one. As it happened, Joseph was present. He recognized his brothers, although they did not realize that this stern, powerful Egyptian official was Joseph. Hiding his surprise and pretending not to know them, Joseph asked his brothers brusquely where they had come from and the purpose of their visit.

The brothers replied that they had come from Canaan to buy food. At this point, Joseph recalled the dreams he had had about his brothers treating him as their master. Without revealing his identity, Joseph maintained his aggressive stance and accused them of being spies trying to discover the weaknesses in Egypt's defenses. The brothers denied this, insisting they were "honest men." They said they all belonged to one family and that the youngest was at home and "one is no more."

Joseph pretended not to be convinced by their story and said they must be tested. He told them they could not leave Egypt until their youngest brother had come to the country. One of them, he said, must go back to Canaan and fetch him while the others were detained. Only then would he believe they were not spies. With that, Joseph sent all of them to jail.

✡ Taking a hostage ✡

After three days, Joseph altered his plan. He decided to keep just one of the brothers in custody and allow the others to go home and bring back Benjamin, "so that your words may be verified and that you may not die." While Joseph stood there in their presence, the brothers began to discuss the situation in their own language. They did not realize that Joseph could understand them because he had been using an interpreter.

In their suffering, the brothers reflected that they were being punished for the evil they had inflicted on Joseph. They remembered how, at the time, he had pleaded for his life. As Joseph listened, he was overcome with emotion, turned away, and began to weep. Then he pulled himself together and ordered Simeon, the second oldest brother, to be taken away as a hostage. He ordered his brothers' sacks to be filled with grain and the silver they had brought as payment to be placed inside them. He also provided food for their journey before sending them on their way.

Grain is distributed during the famine, as illustrated in this 15th-century Italian painting by Giovanni de Bartolommeo. In the center panel, Joseph's brothers visit Egypt to buy grain for their family, not realizing that their brother was in charge.

At an overnight stop on the return journey, one of the brothers discovered some silver in his sack. In alarm, they wondered "what is this that God has done to us?" When they arrived home and had told their father what had happened, they opened their sacks to find that all their silver had been returned. Jacob then lamented that not only had he been deprived of Joseph and Simeon, but now he risked the possibility of losing Benjamin, too. Despite Reuben's promise that he would be prepared to forfeit the lives of his own two sons to ensure Benjamin's safe return, Jacob refused to let Benjamin go: "If harm comes to him on the journey you are taking, you will bring my gray head down to the grave in sorrow."

✡ Foreigners from Canaan ✡

Joseph's first encounter with his brothers in at least 20 years marked the start of his reconciliation with them. With the implication that they were being guided by divine providence, the brothers arrived in an area of Egypt where Joseph happened to be supervising the sale of grain. Travelers from Canaan would have entered the country by its delta region, and it is possible the brothers may have then gone south to Memphis, near modern Cairo. Memphis was the Egyptian capital in the early second millennium BC – the approximate period for the story's setting.

A scribe records grain being stored, in this 18th-century BC Egyptian model of a granary. Because of the huge volume of grain stored, Joseph abandoned record-keeping.

Irrigated agricultural fields in the Nile delta in Egypt are tended by laborers. Each year the river overflowed its banks and the water covered the surrounding land with silt. This made the soil particularly rich for growing crops.

Although Joseph recognized his brothers, it would have been much harder for them to identify someone who, as they imagined, was either enslaved or dead. In addition, Joseph acted the part of a high-born Egyptian and spoke to them through an interpreter, and his costly clothes and his face – clean-shaven in the Egyptian manner – had changed him beyond recognition.

✿ Behind the plan ✿

Joseph's tactic of accusing his brothers of being spies was part of his plan to keep them in the country and find out more about them. But this accusation was not implausible in the light of Egyptian history during the middle of the second millennium BC. Semitic peoples did, in fact, infiltrate the delta region from the east; and, in the 17th century, they took over the country. Ruling from about 1663 to 1555 BC, these people were

known to the Egyptians as the Hyksos, the "Desert Princes."

The only way the brothers could verify their story, Joseph said, was by bringing Benjamin to Egypt. Meanwhile, he jailed them for three days – ample time for the brothers to appreciate the gravity of their predicament and to express their guilt over their past treatment of Joseph. It is only here that Genesis discloses that Joseph had pleaded for his life when thrown into the cistern, a harrowing detail that 20 intervening years could not erase from the brothers' consciences. Listening to his brothers speak, Joseph, it seems, was almost ready to reveal himself and forgive them. Still, however, he was not totally convinced of their change of heart, and he was determined to see the brother he was closest to, Benjamin.

> ❝ 'Your servants were 12 brothers, the sons of one man, who lives in the land of Canaan.' ❞
> GENESIS 42:13

So, except for Simeon, he sent them all back to Canaan. His gifts of food and the return of the silver were hints to his brothers that his aggression was not what it seemed. But his brothers could only see the returned silver as a disconcerting act of God (Genesis 42:28), and they, along with Jacob, were frightened. Indeed, Jacob's reaction to the affair portrays him not as a strong patriarchal figure, calm in a crisis, but as a feeble old man, thinking of his own plight and unable to be constructive. He cared most that he did not have to part with Benjamin, who – so he thought – was his only remaining son by his beloved Rachel.

At the same time, however, the crisis was having a positive effect. The brothers suffered true remorse over Joseph, and Reuben even selflessly volunteered to vouch for the safety of Benjamin to and from Egypt. Jacob still refused: it would take the continuing famine and the threat of death to his entire family to change his mind. ▲

MESSAGE
—for—
TODAY

JOSEPH'S BROTHERS *did not expect to be reminded of their past misdeeds while seeking food supplies in Egypt. But when told they would have to bring Benjamin, their youngest brother, to Egypt, they immediately interpreted the demand as a punishment for their maltreatment of Joseph. It is clear that as much as two decades later, they still felt guilty and related any setback to their sin.*

In Genesis, and throughout the Bible, a strong ethos of reward and punishment is exhibited. Wrongdoers may not suffer in material terms, but they do in other ways – they carry a sense of guilt, a fear about what the future will bring, and an inability to walk in good conscience or sleep easily at night. Those who have tried to live honestly are free from these burdens, a clear lesson in the spiritual consequences of our life choices.

The BROTHERS RETURN to EGYPT

JOSEPH REVEALS *his* IDENTITY
GENESIS 43–45

> **"** *So when they had eaten all the grain they had brought from Egypt, their father said to them, 'Go back and buy us a little more food.'* **"**
> GENESIS 43:2

A S THE FAMINE CONTINUED to grip Canaan, Jacob's family ate all the grain brought back from Egypt. So Jacob told his sons they must return to Egypt and bring back more food. Speaking on behalf of his brothers, Judah replied that unless they brought Benjamin with them, the Egyptian official who was holding Simeon in custody would not see them. He added that he would personally guarantee Benjamin's safety.

Although he was loath to let his beloved Benjamin leave home, Jacob reluctantly agreed. He told his sons to take with them gifts of balm, honey, spices, myrrh, almonds, and pistachio nuts, as well as a double amount of silver to compensate for the silver that had been returned to them after their first visit to Egypt.

Jacob's sons "hurried down to Egypt." They approached the same Egyptian official – Joseph – who told his steward to look after them. Still feeling anxious about the silver that had been returned to them, the brothers confessed their unease to the steward, who told them not to worry, that their God had given them this treasure. The steward then brought out Simeon and provided water for washing their feet and fodder for their donkeys. When Joseph arrived, the brothers gave him the gifts and bowed down before him – as his dreams had foretold.

Joseph inquired about the welfare of their father. Then, spotting Benjamin, his younger brother, he felt a rush of emotion and had to hurry from the room. As soon as he had recovered, he returned and ordered food to be served to them all.

✡ Brothers reunited ✡

After the meal, Joseph ordered his officials to fill his brothers' sacks with food, to put inside them the silver they had brought, and to place his own personal silver cup in Benjamin's sack. After the brothers left for Canaan, Joseph sent his steward to accuse them of stealing the cup. They were shocked and said that if one of them was found guilty, that person would forfeit his life, and the others would become Joseph's slaves.

The steward began to search the sacks and discovered the cup in Benjamin's sack. Baffled and distraught, they all returned to Egypt to face Joseph's wrath. When they arrived, Joseph insisted that Benjamin should become his slave but that the rest of them could go free. But Judah intervened and implored him to let Benjamin go. He said that it would break his father's heart if his youngest son did not return. He offered to be Joseph's slave in his brother's place.

As Joseph listened to Judah's pleas, he was unable keep up the pretense any longer. He

dismissed everyone but his brothers from the room and broke down in sobs. He finally announced to them that he was their brother Joseph. The brothers stared at him in terror. But Joseph told them not to be distressed for selling him into slavery. God had sent him ahead of them into Egypt, he said, so that he could save lives. He said they should return to their father Jacob and urge him to bring his household to Goshen in the fertile Nile delta, because there were five years of famine yet to come. Then, with tears in his eyes, he embraced them, one by one.

A distraught Jacob is unwilling to part with his youngest son Benjamin, in this 19th-century painting by Adolphe Roger. Benjamin's brothers took him to Egypt.

When Pharaoh heard about Joseph and his brothers, he was delighted by their reunion and endorsed Joseph's proposal that his family should immigrate to Egypt. So, laden with food and gifts, the brothers returned to Canaan. They explained to their father that Joseph was alive and, in fact, ruling Egypt. At first, Jacob could not believe it. But when he heard them describe what

Colorful spices are displayed at a modern-day market in Egypt. The spices were valued by the Egyptians, who used them in food preparation, medicine, and cosmetics and for temple rituals. They were also used in embalming (p. 67).

Here modern Palestinians ride their donkeys sidesaddle to avoid hoisting up their garments. Donkeys were used by Joseph's family as well to travel to and from Egypt.

had happened and saw the carts filled with food, he realized it was true. Jacob vowed: "I will go and see him before I die."

✡ *The mysterious official* ✡

The Genesis account of the brothers' second visit to Egypt describes how Joseph continued to manipulate their emotions. When they first arrived at Joseph's house, they feared that they might be accused of theft – the reason why they so readily confessed to the steward about the return of their silver. They must have thought it odd when the steward – a pagan Egyptian – pronounced that "Your God, the God of your father, has given you treasure in your sacks."

The solicitous hospitality and the appearance of Simeon would have been reassuring. But at mealtime, they were astonished to find that they had been seated in order of their ages – there was no one among the Egyptians who would have known how old they were. They must also have wondered why Benjamin was served five times as much food as anyone else.

> ❝ They told him, 'Joseph is still alive! In fact, he is ruler of all Egypt.' ❞
>
> GENESIS 45:26

When the brothers left for Canaan, they must have been elated to have rescued Simeon, obtained food, and kept Benjamin safe. But their euphoria turned to despair when the cup was found in Benjamin's sack. Adversity must have forged a spirit of solidarity among them; they stuck together, even though the steward and then Joseph declared that they could all go free except Benjamin. Judah (who had tried to help Joseph previously; pp. 64–67) seemed to personify their new selflessness when he delivered his heart-moving speech, offering himself as a substitute for Benjamin. Judah's words were a turning point for Joseph, who could see that the brothers who had sold him into slavery had been transformed.

Wrenched from happiness to misery, the brothers then had the biggest shock of all: the Egyptian vizier was none other than their long-lost brother. Not only that, but far from bearing any malice, he told them that by selling him into slavery they had been part of God's providential plan to raise him to power and to save lives. Three times Joseph reiterated that it was God who had sent him to Egypt: the Lord had incorporated their evil deed at Dothan into a greater scheme "to preserve for you a remnant on Earth and to save your lives by a great deliverance."

This did not excuse the brothers for their action; they had to bear full responsibility for their crime and earn forgiveness from Joseph by showing genuine repentance. Nevertheless, in creating good out of evil, God was asserting His sovereign rule over people's lives. ▲

MESSAGE
—for—
TODAY

HOW DO YOU KNOW if a person — be it someone else or yourself — has truly repented of a previous wrong? Perhaps by testing how the person reacts when put in the same position again. A person who has repented will act in a positive way the second time.

This is what lies behind Joseph's plot for his brothers. It would have been easy for them to abandon Benjamin — Jacob's new favorite son — to slavery in Egypt, just as they had done with Joseph earlier. This time, however, they acted responsibly, stood up for their brother, and sought to protect both him and their father. Only then did Joseph know they had truly repented, and only when he saw this was Joseph able to forgive them. True repentance means not only apologizing, but changing. It is within all of us to repent; we can learn from our previous mistakes so we can take the right action in the future.

To the LAND of PHARAOH

JACOB MIGRATES to EGYPT
GENESIS 46–47:12

> *Israel said to Joseph, 'Now I am ready to die, since I have seen for myself that you are still alive.'*
> GENESIS 46:30

DETERMINED TO SEE his long-lost son Joseph, Jacob moved his household from Hebron to Egypt. On the way, they stopped at Beersheba, where Jacob offered sacrifices to God. At night, he received a vision from the Lord, who told Jacob not to be frightened to go to Egypt; He would bring him back to Canaan. Reassured, Jacob and his family continued their journey, making use of carts sent by Pharaoh. Judah was sent ahead to warn Joseph of their arrival. Joseph met his family at Goshen, in the Nile delta. As soon as he saw his

Joseph embraces his elderly, bearded father Jacob while his brothers (right) and Egyptian soldiers (left) look on, in this detail from a sixth-century Byzantine ivory chair.

father, Joseph embraced him, weeping with joy. Jacob stated that now, having seen Joseph, he was ready to die.

Joseph told his family what to say to Pharaoh when he interviewed them; they were to stress that they were shepherds, as their ancestors had been. Pharaoh would let them settle in Goshen, because the Egyptians detested "all shepherds" and would not welcome them in their towns.

Joseph brought five of his brothers to Pharaoh, who gave the family freedom to live in Goshen. Joseph then presented his father to the king. Without inhibition, Jacob blessed Pharaoh, who asked him how old he was. Jacob replied that he was 130 years old, but his age did not equal those of his forefathers. Then he blessed the king again. Joseph finally settled his family in Egypt.

✡ Out of the Promised Land ✡

Jacob's migration to Egypt was significant: it meant that Jacob and his family left the land of promise for the land where the children of Israel would be enslaved. Jacob's father Isaac had been forbidden to go to Egypt during a previous famine (Genesis 26:2), but Jacob had the approval of God. He also had motivations: a reunion with Joseph, the prospect of food, and grazing land for his animals. Jacob had doubts about leaving Canaan, but his fears were dispelled at Beersheba, when God gave His assurance that He would bring Jacob back from Egypt. This indicated that Jacob's family would not permanently stay in Egypt: Canaan was still the land of promise.

One reason Jacob's family had to stress that they were shepherds, with their own animals, was to show that there was no threat of their living in town and taking Egyptian jobs. Pharaoh was pleased to let them settle in Goshen, and he had them care for some of his own livestock as well.

When Joseph presented his father to Pharaoh, Jacob took the senior role and blessed the king, instead of bowing low, as expected. Pharaoh could apparently see that God was with Jacob. ▲

MESSAGE
—for—
TODAY

THE PERSON FROM a humble background who rises in society does not always wish to be reminded of his or her origins. This is not so with Joseph. He was not ashamed of his past, and he lost no time in sharing his good fortune with his newly rediscovered family.

Joseph knew that if he cut himself off from his own roots, he would hurt his family (who were looked upon as immigrant shepherds by the Egyptians) and would impoverish himself. Perhaps he sensed that dissociating himself from them would lower his stature in the eyes of the Egyptians: the person who denies his past may one day deny his present. This does not inspire trust. As the Jewish sages put it: "He who runs after popularity will find it runs away from him. Others will respect you only if you are you."

A LAST FAREWELL

The BLESSING of JACOB
GENESIS 47:28–49:28

> *'Nevertheless, his younger brother will be greater than he, and his descendants will become a group of nations.'*
>
> GENESIS 48:19

SEVENTEEN YEARS AFTER moving to Egypt, Jacob – at 147 years of age – sensed that he was coming to the end of his life. So he summoned Joseph to make him swear that after he died, Joseph would see that his body was taken back to Canaan and not buried in Egypt.

Some time later, Jacob fell ill. Joseph hurried with his sons, Manasseh and Ephraim, to see him. Jacob told Joseph how God had blessed him at Bethel (Genesis 28:13), and he restated the promises of the covenant. Jacob said he would count Manasseh and Ephraim as his own children – that is, formally adopt them – and told Joseph to bring them nearer so that he could bless them.

Joseph positioned Manasseh on Jacob's right side – traditionally the place of honor – so he could receive the blessing of the firstborn; he then placed Ephraim on Jacob's left. But Jacob deliberately crossed his hands over and began to give his

The dying Jacob is shown giving his blessing to Joseph's two children, in this 17th-century Dutch painting by Hermensz van Rijn Rembrandt.

blessing. Seeing that Jacob had placed his right hand on Ephraim's head, Joseph tried to reposition it. Jacob resisted, saying that Ephraim would be greater than Manasseh and his descendants would become "a group of nations." He also told Joseph that he was about to die, but he reassured his son that God would take his descendants back to Canaan; then he bequeathed him land in Canaan. Finally, Jacob gave his own sons his blessings.

✡ The fate of the tribes ✡

Jacob insisted on being buried in the family tomb in Canaan (pp. 30–31). In this way, he would lie next to his ancestors and ensure that his offspring remembered that it was Canaan, not Egypt, that God had promised to them.

In a scene that recalls Isaac blessing Jacob in the belief that he was Esau, Jacob bestowed the blessing of the firstborn on Ephraim and declared that he would become the greater tribe. This prediction came true when Israel was divided into southern and northern kingdoms (930–722 BC). Ephraim became so numerous that the name was used to refer to the northern tribes collectively.

Jacob gave Joseph a bequest of land won from the Amorite people. Because the Hebrew word for this "ridge of land" or "mountain ridge" is *shechem*, some scholars believe Jacob meant the city of Shechem. Conversely, because Jacob had condemned the massacre at Shechem (pp. 56–59), others believe he was referring to an unrecorded place. In any case, by giving Joseph this land, Jacob ensured that God's pledge of giving Canaan to his descendants would be fulfilled.

The 12 blessings were given in poetic, sometimes opaque, language. Although his pronouncements are known as the "blessings of Jacob," they are a mixture of blessings and predictions – some of them negative – of what would befall his sons and the 12 tribes of Israel descended from them in Canaan. At heart, Jacob's predictions presented a future in which the tribes would take their place in the land God had pledged to them. ▲

MESSAGE
—for—
TODAY

IT IS THE YOUNGER CHILD who receives the main blessing, with Ephraim favored instead of Manasseh. This mirrors Jacob's own story – when he took his father's blessing from his older brother Esau – and is a constant theme in the Bible. The eldest may have certain rights of inheritance, but religious leadership is not hereditary; it requires character. Thus it was Moses who took precedence over his older brother, and the youngest son, David, who was chosen by Samuel as the anointed one.

Religious merit depends on who you are and what you stand for. The second-century Rabbi Simon declared, "Admire most not those who have inherited much, but who have created much and wear the crown of a good reputation." We may have to change our character for the better before being worthy of God's blessing.

The END of an ERA

The DEATHS of JACOB and JOSEPH

GENESIS 49:29–50

" *Pharaoh said, 'Go up and bury your father, as he made you swear to do.'* **"**

GENESIS 50:6

A FTER JACOB HAD blessed his sons, he told them to bury him in the cave of Machpelah (pp. 30–31), where his father and grandfather had been buried. Then, drawing his feet up into the bed, he "breathed his last." Filled with grief, Joseph embraced his father's lifeless body and wept. When he had sufficiently recovered, he made arrangements for Jacob's corpse to be embalmed, so that it would not decompose before the time came when it could be buried in Canaan.

Such had been Jacob's standing among the Egyptians that they mourned him for 70 days. Afterward, Pharaoh gave Joseph permission to fulfill his oath to take his father's body to Canaan. Joseph and his family (but not his children) set out with a cavalcade of Egyptian officials and horsemen. Their route probably took them across the Sinai

The burial of Jacob is depicted in this 15th-century illustration from the Nuremberg Bible *in Germany. Jacob's body was taken to the family tomb in Canaan.*

Peninsula, then northward to the east of the Dead Sea. When they came to a place called Afad, near the Jordan River, they stopped and mourned Jacob for seven days. Finally, they entered Canaan and arrived at the cave of Machpelah, where they laid Jacob in the tomb. Joseph, his brothers, and the rest of the company then returned to Egypt.

With their father no longer alive, Joseph's brothers worried that Joseph might avenge himself for their crime against him many years before. So they sent him a message saying that before Jacob died, he had instructed them to ask Joseph for his forgiveness. When Joseph received their message, he wept – but whether he did so because his brothers had in fear resorted to fabricating a story or because they still mistrusted his forgiveness is unclear. Regardless, his brothers then offered themselves as his slaves, but Joseph reassured them that the harm they had done had been used by God to save lives.

Joseph continued to live in Egypt with his family. As he approached death, Joseph made his brothers swear to take his body back to Canaan. Joseph passed away at the age of 110. After he died, his body, like Jacob's, was embalmed. It was placed in a coffin in Egypt, ready to eventually be taken to Canaan.

✡ At rest in Canaan ✡

By burying Jacob's body in Canaan, Jacob's sons were renewing their claim to the land, serving notice that they or their descendants would one day return there.

Genesis ends by looking forward to another beginning when Joseph's brothers swore they would take his body to Canaan. Years later, Moses would lead the Israelites out of Egypt, taking with them Joseph's remains (Exodus 13:19). In time, the Israelites would invade Canaan and bury Joseph at Shechem, in the plot of land Jacob had bought (Genesis 33:19). As the Lord had pledged to Abraham, Isaac, and Jacob, the children of Israel would come home to the Promised Land. ▲

MESSAGE
—for—
TODAY

THE DEATH OF JACOB caused his sons great insecurity about their own future. Might Joseph now take vengeance on them for the way they had treated him as a boy? The message that they claimed was from Jacob – that Joseph should not harm them – was almost certainly their own invention in a desperate attempt to protect themselves.

Joseph had assured his brothers of his forgiveness of their previous misdeeds, but they could not completely accept his goodwill. Joseph had put the past behind him, and he was no longer weighed down by it. As a result, he was much freer than his brothers. Those who hang onto suspicion and enmity harm themselves more than others. By letting go of any baser emotions, Joseph was able to accept his brothers with confidence and goodwill.

ABOUT *the* PEOPLES

THE PATRIARCHS, as recorded in Genesis, often encountered other peoples, or tribes. Here is a brief history of their own people and those that they met in their travels.

HEBREWS

The Patriarchs – Abraham, Isaac, and Jacob – were members of a Semitic nomadic tribe; the people probably became known as Hebrew in Abraham's time. The Semitic tribes in Mesopotamia worshiped within a polytheistic religion. Their chief deity was the storm god Shaddai, the equivalent of the Canaanite deity Ba'al. With Abraham's belief in the Lord, a monotheistic faith and the foundations of Judaism were laid.

As part of his religious ritual, Abraham erected altars and sacrificed animals in those places where he had communicated with God. The Hebrews disapproved of the Canaanites' worship of idols and saw these practices as degenerate.

CANAANITES

The Canaanites were the settled inhabitants of Canaan and southern Syria, which was populated in 3000 BC. In the Bible these people are identified as descendants of Canaan, a son of Ham and a grandson of Noah. The country was made up of independent city-states, each with its own ruler and aristocracy. It was a sophisticated and wealthy society that had written records from as early as 2000 BC. Its economy was based on the export of manufactured goods such as metalwork and textiles. When the Hebrews arrived in Canaan, they forced the Canaanites to accept them.

The Canaanites' religion focused on fertility because they were dependent on the success of their harvests. El was at the center of the Canaanite pantheon, but the most popular deities were Ba'al, the god of fertility (p. 50), and the fertility goddess Astarte. Among the religious rites were sexual rituals, to encourage fertility of the land and livestock, and human sacrifice, believed to please the gods. The Old Testament condemned the moral depravity of this religion and forbade the Hebrews' participation in it.

HITTITES

Originally from beyond the Black Sea, the Hittite kingdom was based in Central Anatolia. The name of the people came from previous inhabitants of the area, the Hatti. The Hittites were powerful in the Near East beginning in 2000 BC, and by 1300 BC, they held the region of Syria. Their expansion created conflicts with others, especially the Egyptians. The Hittite Empire's power had declined by 1200 BC, because of the invasion of the Sea Peoples, a group of marauders sometimes identified with the Philistines.

The Hittites believed that their king was the earthly deputy for their storm god. As in Egyptian practice, they recognized the king as the intermediary between the gods and his subjects, and therefore divinely protected. The king's role as chief priest of the gods came before his military, administrative, and judicial duties. It was his duty to placate the deity in order to protect his nation. The Hittites worshiped other Anatolian deities, as well as Syrian and Hurrian divinities.

EGYPTIANS

In about 3100 BC, Egypt, which comprised two principal areas, the delta in the north and the Nile valley in the south, was united by a king named Menes. This began the line of pharaohs that endured for 30 dynasties and 30 centuries. At the height of its power, Egypt's empire extended from the Euphrates River in Syria to the Fourth Cataract of the Nile River in Nubia. Egypt owed its success both to the fertility of the land and to the cultural achievements of a great civilization. Its prosperity declined by 332 BC, when it was conquered by Alexander the Great.

The Egyptians explained the world around them with a religion encompassing many gods.

The Beni Hasan tomb painting (c. 1895 BC) depicts Semitic traders bringing goods, including eye paint, to the Egyptians. The original painting is shown right and a reconstruction below and left. The Egyptians are wrapped in white linen cloths and the Semites are enrobed in brightly colored tunics.

According to their beliefs, primal waters called Nun existed before the world was created. From this chaos rose the sun god Ra, who was responsible for the birth of all other deities, each of whom had a role related to Egyptian life and death.

The pharaoh was believed to be the living link between his subjects and the gods. During his life he was the incarnation of Horus, the sky god, who was the son of Isis and Osiris. In death the pharaoh merged with the ruler of the dead, Osiris. The association of immortal rulers with the pharaohs on Earth enhanced the kings' authority, and subjects often expressed their devotion to the gods through homage paid to their temporal ruler. When a king died his body was mummified and placed in a tomb. This recalled the embalming of Osiris's body by his wife and sister Isis and the jackal-headed god, Anubis.

Ordinary people worshiped household gods, including Taweret, a goddess who protected pregnant women, and Bes, the dwarf god of the family. Each region worshiped its own local gods. ▲

CUSTOMS *and* MANNERS

THE EVERYDAY HABITS of the people in the time of Genesis have been well documented. Here is a brief insight into how they worked and lived.

AGRICULTURE

Canaanite agriculture depended on three crops: grains, grapes, and olives. The two most important grains were wheat and barley, although millet was grown as well. The crops depended on the fall and spring rains, without which the ground could not be plowed or seeds sown. Vineyards were planted to produce fresh and dried grapes and to make wine, while olive groves produced the oil that was so crucial to the Hebrews' diet. Olive oil was also necessary to fuel lamps and played an integral part in many religious rituals.

People kept their records on stone tablets, plotting the course of the crops and the seasons, such as on this agricultural limestone calendar found at Gezer (left).

TOOLS

Standing grain was cut using sickles. In early times the tool would have been made from wood or even the jawbone of a large animal. The stalks were cut near the top and the remainder left in the ground for the sheep to graze on. Separating the grain and straw was handled in two ways: threshing was done by using a flail (a long flexible stick); winnowing was carried out by using a five-pronged fork (winnowing fan) and a spade (winnowing shovel).

Although the seminomadic life of the Canaanites did not lead to great skills in carpentry, they did have a basic knowledge of woodwork. The ax and saw were standard tools used. Initially, the ax head was made from bronze (above, right) and

lashed to a wooden handle, and the saw was produced from ribbon flints set into a wood frame. Later, metal blades were used for the saw and iron for the ax head. Chisels, mallets, and adzes were used for more delicate carpentry.

SHEPHERDING

Sheep and goats provided meat, wool, milk, and horn containers. For these early people, real wealth did not lie in jewelry but in herds: sheep to provide clothing and goats to provide food and milk or to exchange for money or goods. Often the responsibility for the sheep and goats of a whole village would be given to one shepherd.

HUNTING

In the mountains of Lebanon and Syria and the valley of the Jordan River, wild animals were plentiful; the meat from herds of animals, including oryx, antelopes, and gazelles, was supplemented by that from other game animals. The bow and arrow was used in the hunt, but hunters typically dug pits to trap large animals and caught birds and small prey with nets. In Egypt and later in Assyria, hunting became a sport. The Assyrian kings held lion hunts in royal game reserves.

BAKING

Bread was a staple part of the diet. Barley or wheat grain was ground, using a pestle and mortar or a hand mill consisting of two stones (right). The lower stone held the grain, while the upper stone was rubbed or

rolled across the bed of grain to make the flour. Water and salt were then added; if the bread was to be leavened, some fermented dough from the previous day's bread was added too. The dough was placed in a convex dish over the fire or in an earthenware receptacle or primitive oven to bake.

MUSIC AND MUSICIANS

In the same class as smiths and those who possessed herds, musicians played an important part in Hebrew society. "Theory tablets" with instructions on how to tune instruments have been found dating from 1800 BC. Instruments were played at family parties; song and dance celebrated the return of war heroes; kings were enthroned to music; and music was played at royal courts. Workers sang as they performed their tasks, and many occupations used music to pace their actions. Among the main instruments were the ram's horn, double pipe (left), flute, lyre, harp, tambourine, and cymbals. The accent on rhythm in traditional Hebrew music shows how music and dancing were strongly linked to each other.

HOSPITALITY

The nomadic existence of peoples of the Bible instilled in them an urge to be hospitable. This was reinforced by divine sanction: it was a sin to refuse to share food with the needy. Strangers would be invited to spend the night and members of the family would often sleep with the visitor, because it was believed to be discourteous to leave a person without company through the night.

BEDS AND PILLOWS

The beds for the poor were simple mats or a few folds of clothing spread out on the floor. Some homes had raised earthen benches or platforms built along a wall. For the daytime, the mat that served as a bed was rolled up and put away, and the platform was used for sitting. Only the wealthy could afford a separate bed or bed-chamber. Some of the very wealthy had beds made of wooden frames inlaid with ivory, gold, and silver, which also doubled as couches on which to recline when feasting. For a pillow, people might use a roll of clothing or even a stone, though some pillows were more lavish, such as the neck rest (above). Beds also had a role in death – on occasion they served as funeral biers.

EDUCATION

When Abraham left Ur in Sumer, he was leaving a highly civilized city. Schools in Ur taught language, mathematics, geography, botany, and drawing and trained people for religious, commercial, and governmental work.

When the Hebrew people moved into the desert, they didn't have a sophisticated education system. It evolved as their civilization did and was influenced by surrounding nations. Education was centered in the home, with the child's father teaching children from three years of age. He taught them the Law and often a trade. All education was influenced heavily by religion.

GAMES

Many games and leisure activities were seen as a means of shaping bodies and minds. Board games were popular: one of the oldest games known is the Royal Game of Ur (below), which was played in 1800 BC. Other board games were similar to chess, and some games were played with dice – either a two-sided die in the form of a disk or a four-sided die in the shape of a pyramid. ▲

BIBLIOGRAPHY

Aharoni, Yohanan *The Land of the Bible.* Westminster Press, Philadelphia, 1979

Albright, William F. *The Archaeology of Palestine.* Penguin Books, Harmondsworth, England, 1949

Alexander, D., Alexander, P. (eds.) *The Lion Handbook to the Bible.* Lion Publishing, Berkhamstead, 1973

Anderson, Bernard W. *The Living World of the Old Testament.* Longman, London, 1978

Baldwin, Joyce G. *The Message of Genesis 12–50.* Inter-Varsity Press, Leicester, England, 1986

Bright, John *A History of Israel.* Westminster Press, Philadelphia, 1972

Frank, Harry T. *An Archaeological Companion to the Bible.* SCM Press, London, 1972 – *Discovering the Biblical World.* Hodder & Stoughton, London, 1975

Gardner, Joseph L. (ed.) *Atlas of the Bible.* Reader's Digest, New York, 1981

Gibson, John C.L. *Genesis: Volume 2.* The Westminster Press, Philadelphia, 1982

Gower, Ralph *The New Manners and Customs of Bible Times.* Moody Press, Chicago, 1987

Grollenberg, L.H. *The Penguin Shorter Atlas of the Bible.* Penguin Books, Harmondsworth, England, 1978

Heaton, E.W. *Everyday Life in Old Testament Times.* Charles Scribner, New York, 1956

Keller, Werner *The Bible as History.* BCA, London, 1974

Kidner, Derek *Genesis: An Introduction and Commentary.* The Tyndale Press, London, 1967

McGrath, Alister *NIV Bible Commentary.* Hodder & Stoughton, London, 1995

May, Herbert G. *Oxford Bible Atlas.* Oxford University Press, Oxford, 1974

Metzger, B., Goldstein, D., Ferguson, J. (eds.) *Great Events of Bible Times.* Weidenfeld and Nicolson, London, 1987

Parker, Geoffrey (ed.) *The Times Atlas of World History.* Times Books, London, 1993

Porter, J.R. *The Illustrated Guide to the Bible.* Oxford University Press, Oxford, 1995

Richards, Lawrence O. *The Applied Bible Dictionary.* Kingsway Publications, 1990

Rogerson, John *The New Atlas of the Bible.* Macdonald & Co., London, 1985

Wenham, Gordon J. *World Biblical Commentary: Genesis 16–50.* Word Books, Dallas, Texas, 1994

INDEX

Page numbers in **bold** denote main mentions; numbers in *italics* refer to illustrations and their captions; *mp* and *M* indicate maps and the Message for Today box, respectively.

ACKNOWLEDGMENTS

ILLUSTRATION

David Atkinson (maps); Debbie Hinks (illustration symbols).

PICTURE CREDITS

l = left, **r** = right, **t** = top, **c** = center, **b** = bottom
1 Laura Lushington/Sonia Halliday Photographs; 2–3 Sonia Halliday Photographs; 3 San Petronio, Italy/Bridgeman Art Library; 5 AKG London; 8 Erich Lessing/AKG London; 10 Bridgeman Art Library; 13 AKG London; 14t John Dewar/ Sonia Halliday Photographs, 14b Sonia Halliday Photographs; 17 Tretyakov Gallery, Moscow/AKG London; 18 British Library, London/Bridgeman Art Library; 19 ASAP/Robert Harding Picture Library; 21 Rafael Valls Gallery, London/Bridgeman Art Library; 22 Sonia Halliday Photographs; 23 Barry Searle/Sonia Halliday Photographs; 24 Musée des Beaux-Arts, Tours/Peter Willi/Bridgeman Art Library; 27 Musée Conde, Chantilly/Giraudon/Bridgeman Art Library; 28 Magyar Nemzeti Galeria, Budapest/Bridgeman Art Library; 29 Musée du Louvre, Paris/Erich Lessing/AKG London; 30 Sonia Halliday Photographs; 33 Musée du Louvre, Paris/Erich Lessing/AKG London; 34 E.T. Archive; 35 Laura Lushington/Sonia Halliday Photographs; 6 Bridgeman Art Library; 39 Caylus Anticuario, Madrid/Bridgeman Art Library; 40 British Museum, London/Erich Lessing/AKG London; 41 Ancient Art & Architecture Collection; 42 Lambeth Palace Library, London/Bridgeman Art Library; 45 Erich Lessing/AKG London;

46–47 Sonia Halliday Photographs; 49 Vatican Museums & Galleries, Rome/AKG London; 50 E.T. Archive; 50–51 Sonia Halliday Photographs; 52–57 AKG London; 58l Ancient Art & Architecture Collection, 58r Erich Lessing/AKG London; 60 Erich Lessing/AKG London; 61 Staatliche Museen, Berlin/Bridgeman Art Library; 62, 65 Staatlich Museen, Berline/Bridgeman Art Library; 66l Erich Lessing/AKG London, 66r Burghley House, Stamford/Bridgeman Art Library; 68 Holkham Hall, Norfolk/Fitzwilliam Museum, University of Cambridge/Bridgeman Art Library; 71 Musée des Beaux-Arts, Rouen/Giraudon/ Bridgeman Art Library; 72-3 Erich Lessing/AKG London; 75 Fitzwilliam Museum, University of Cambridge/ Bridgeman Art Library; 76t British Museum/ Michael Holford, 77b James Strachan/Tony Stone; 79 Musée des Beaux-Arts, Rouen/Peter Willi/Bridgeman Art Library; 80t Robert Harding Picture Library, 80b Michael Good/Impact; 82 E.T. Archive; 84 Gemaldegalerie, Kassel/Bridgeman Art Library; 86 Private Collection/Bridgeman Art Library; 88–89 Peter Clayton; 90l and 90tr Erich Lessing/AKG London, 90br Michael Holford; 91t and 91c Erich Lessing/AKG London, 91b Ancient Art & Architecture Collection; 96 Lauros-Giraudon/Bridgeman Art Library.

If the publishers have unwittingly infringed copyright in any of the illustrations reproduced, they would pay an apppropriate fee on being satisfied of the owner's title.

Anubis, the jackal-headed Egyptian god of the dead, embalms a corpse, in this 13th-century BC Egyptian tomb painting. Both Jacob and Joseph were embalmed in the Egyptian manner.